D1601617

000000443

Aristophanes, 3: The Suits, Clouds, Birds (Pen

Penn Greek Drama Series

Series Editors
David R. Slavitt
Palmer Bovie

The Penn Greek Drama Series presents fresh literary translations of the entire corpus of classical Greek drama: tragedies, comedies, and satyr plays. The only contemporary uniform series of all the surviving work of Aeschylus, Sophocles, Euripides, Aristophanes, and Menander, this collection brings together men and women of literary distinction whose versions of the plays in contemporary English poetry can be acted on the stage or in the individual reader's theater of the mind.

The aim of the series is to make this cultural treasure accessible, restoring as faithfully as possible the original luster of the plays and offering in living verse a view of what talented contemporary poets have seen in their readings of these works so fundamental a part of Western civilization.

Aristophanes, 3

The Suits, Clouds, Birds

Edited by
David R. Slavitt *a n d* Palmer Bovie

PENN

University of Pennsylvania Press
Philadelphia

10 9 8 7 6 5 4 3 2 1

Published by
University of Pennsylvania Press
Philadelphia, Pennsylvania 19104-4011

Library of Congress Cataloging-in-Publication Data
Aristophanes.
    [Works. English. 1998]
    Aristophanes / edited by David R. Slavitt and Palmer Bovie
      p.   cm. — (Penn Greek drama series)
    Contents: 1. The Acharnians. Peace. Celebrating ladies. Wealth—
2. Wasps. Lysistrata. Frogs. The Sexual congress—3. The Suits. Clouds. Birds
    ISBN 0-8122-3456-1 (v. 1 : cloth : acid-free paper).—ISBN 0-8122-1662-8
(v. 1 : pbk. : acid-free paper).—ISBN 0-8122-3483-9 (v. 2 : cloth : acid-free
paper).—ISBN 0-8122-1684-9 (v. 2 : pbk. : acid-free paper).—ISBN 0-8122-
3501-0 (v. 3 : cloth : acid-free paper).—ISBN 0-8122-1698-9 (v. 2 : pbk. : acid-
free paper)
    1. Aristophanes—Translations into English.   2. Greek drama
(Comedy)—Translations into English.   I. Slavitt, David R., 1935–   .
II. Bovie, Smith Palmer.   III. Title.   IV. Series.
PA3877.A1S58   1998
882′.01—dc21   98-8446
                                               CIP

Contents

Introduction

Ralph M. Rosen

The plays of Aristophanes collected in these volumes, composed and performed in Athens during the fifth and fourth centuries B.C., are the earliest surviving record of comic drama in Western culture. Like its contemporary and cognate form tragedy, Attic comedy seems to appear suddenly as a fully formed and remarkably complex poetic genre, paradoxically wedded to its own cultural moment yet profoundly resonant for audiences and readers up to our own time. Indeed, the seeds of Gilbert and Sullivan, the Marx Brothers, or Monty Python's Flying Circus are readily apparent in Aristophanes and can easily lead one to assume that not much has changed in comedy since antiquity. Yet the comic drama of fifth-century Athens, known as Old Comedy, was the product of a long and complex process of literary and cultural interactions and displays as many idiosyncrasies of its own age as it does links to later traditions. Behind the sprightly, colloquial translations featured in this series lie a richly varied Greek verse form and, as the following pages will show, a comic aesthetic by turns alien and familiar to our own sensibilities.

Twice a year during the fifth century the Athenians would gather together to honor Dionysus, god of wine and revelry. The largest and most extravagant occurred in early spring, toward the end of March, and was known as the Great Dionysia, or City Dionysia, to distinguish it from the so-called rural Dionysia, which were celebrated on a lesser scale throughout the Attic countryside. The other festival was known as the Lenaean Dionysia (named after the Lenaion sanctuary where it was held), a more limited, domestic affair that took place in January–February. Various activities occurred at these festivals, including processions, sacrifices, and musical competitions, but the central event at each was the performance of tragedy and comedy. Great expense and effort were lavished on these dramatic performances, as poets and actors competed for prizes awarded by a panel of judges drawn from ten tribes of Attica.

Tragedy and comedy were so much a part of a formal state event that the entire Athenian citizenry might, in principle, attend the performances. The Theater of Dionysus itself on the Athenian acropolis was evidently capable of holding about 17,000 spectators. The Lenaean Dionysia was a smaller and less prestigious affair than the City Dionysia, and theatrical performances were formalized there rather late in the century (about 440 B.C.). Even so, the Lenaea was as public an event as the City Dionysia, and the plots of Lenaean tragedy and comedy likewise reflect the poets' awareness that they were composing before the entire "national" community.

Drawing on a rich store of inherited myths and plots, the most skillful tragic poets crafted plays that could address issues central to Athenian political and social ideology—the relationship between rulers and their subjects, the nature of democracy, the interaction of man and woman, to name a few—and the result was that characteristically "tragic" blend of timeliness and universalizing. Greek comedy evolved alongside tragedy at the festival competitions and became equally implicated in its own historical moment, but, unlike tragedy, it was not constrained to work with mythological material, nor did it need to preserve a consistent and unbroken dramatic illusion. The comic poet was relatively free to invent plots out of whole cloth, and his imagination was limited only by his sense of what the audience would find acceptable. Furthermore, although it shared with tragedy basic compositional units, namely the alternation of spoken "episodes" with choral song and dance, comic diction was far less formal and stylized than that of tragedy. Old Comedy, therefore, could reflect the contemporary cultural climate much more directly than could tragedy: not only could the poet allude to current events or famous people through allegory or analogy but he could even name names, express indignation, and claim a personal authority (however disingenuously) to a degree wholly unavailable to his colleagues in tragedy.

The license afforded Attic comedy in the composition of plots and choice of language has a history that extends well beyond its institutionalization at the Dionysian festivals of fifth-century Athens. The exact origins of Attic comedy are difficult to trace, but the word *komoidia* itself, from which "comedy" derives, offers a useful starting point. *Komoidia* means a *komos*-song, where the *komos* refers to a group of men, often costumed, who entertained audiences with song and dance at various festive occasions. Modern analogues to the ancient *komos* are likely to be found in the activities of Mummers, still common in certain European and American holiday celebrations. Like Mummers, *komos*-singers (*komoidoi*) performed interactively with an audience, often humorously cajoling and mocking individuals with attitudes and language that in normal circumstances would be disruptive and transgressive. Little is known about how and when *komoi* actually became comic drama, formally performed before a passive audience, but the most fundamental vestige of the *komoi* in Attic comedy can be seen in the humorously antagonistic relationships so common between individual characters and groups of characters, and between poet and audience. Fifth-century comic drama preserves some of the carnivalesque spirit of the *komos*, which rendered vituperation and satirical commentary innocuous by means of humor, irony, and a basic assumption that comic speech was ultimately fictive, no matter how "real" it pretended to be in performance.

Indeed, perhaps the central dynamic of Aristophanic comedy is precisely the tension that arises between the poet's voice, with its didactic claims and autobiographical pretenses, and the fictional demands of the genre itself. Did Aristophanes write the *Clouds*, which satirizes Socrates and his followers, because he had a genuine personal animus against him, or because Socrates was an eccentric, funny-looking man who would make a great comic spectacle? Or did the poet exploit the comic potential of Socrates, not because he had anything against him personally but because he wanted to use him to register his own sincere criticism of current philosophical trends? That seems reasonable until one notes that the play itself offers very little in the way of philosophical consistency: traditional "philosophy," which the play ostensibly endorses, ends up as comically ridiculous as the newfangled, sophistic ways that it claims to repudiate through its satirizing of Socrates.

We face a similar dilemma in assessing Aristophanes' relationship with his other famous target, the demagogic politician Cleon, who is relentlessly, often violently, mocked in *The Suits*, and mentioned with disdain at least somewhere in nearly all his fifth-century plays. Aristophanes even alludes to an actual personal feud with Cleon, a feud that supposedly began when Cleon attempted to prosecute the poet for publicly ridiculing Athenian politicians in his (now lost) play of 426 B.C., *Babylonians*. Aristophanes was very convincing: ancient commentators spoke of the feud as if it were a documented historical fact, and modern critics have followed suit, even though our only evidence ultimately comes from the comedies themselves, which have a generic obligation to create personal animosities between the poet and a target. We will probably never know for sure whether Aristophanes truly feuded with Cleon, but the question of historicity is ultimately less significant than the ways the comic poet persistently exploited the topos throughout his plays. For through the relationship with Cleon as it was developed on the stage over several plays spanning at least five years—*The Acharnians* (425), *The Suits* (424), *Clouds* (423), *Wasps* (422), and *Peace* (421)—Aristophanes could dramatize with brilliant economy the ethos of boisterous confrontation and antagonism that fueled so many plays of Attic comedy.

Any literature in which an author adopts a stance of moral indignation and undeserved beleaguerment and engages in invective or personal mockery makes it especially difficult for the audience to separate fiction from reality, if only because the author works hard to enlist their sympathies for his allegedly urgent and topical predicament. Yet despite this implied bond with an audience in opposition to a target, a group, or even an issue, we never witness the poet's voice directly in any of Aristophanes' plays (Dikaiopolis in *The Acharnians*, is about as close as we get to this). No character ever explicitly represents the poet himself, and the poet's name is never directly mentioned. Instead, Aristophanes avails himself of a structural device known as the *parabasis*, which had become the conventional place in Old Comedy where the poet could interrupt the flow of episodes and make personal claims through the mouthpiece of the chorus. The parabasis, which comes from the verb *parabaino*, "to step aside," was essentially a digression, a temporary halt in the main action while the chorus came forward to address the audience. Its location in the play was not rigidly fixed but tended to occur toward the middle of the play, often functioning as a kind of entr'acte. In its most elaborate form—as we see, for example, in *Wasps*—the parabasis consists of a prolonged exchange between the chorus and their leader, alternating spoken and sung verse, in which the chorus leader actually speaks on behalf of the poet.

Through the chorus leader, then, Aristophanes could take up any number of topics, including current events, the superiority of his comedy over that of his rivals, indignation at the audience for lack of support, and, of course, abuse against "personal enemies" such as Cleon. The parabasis is our main source for "autobiographical" information about Aristophanes and the primary reason it has always been so tempting to take a biographical approach to the interpretation of Aristophanes. When *Clouds* makes fun of Socrates or *The Suits* inveighs against Cleon, when Aeschylus defeats Euripides in the literary contest of *Frogs*, the relationship with the audience that Aristophanes establishes in successive parabases makes it easy to assume that the plots themselves functioned likewise as a coded, didactic message: Aeschylus defeated Euripides, so Aristophanes must therefore endorse this verdict and be trying to warn us against the evils of Euripides! But if *Frogs*, to continue with this example, were such a simplistic morality play, Aristophanes would hardly have ridiculed the literary excesses of *both* tragic poets with as much care as he does, nor would he have left the final decision to the waffling, delightfully buffoonish god Dionysus, who can barely offer a rationale for his final elevation of Aeschylus from the underworld.

Centuries of readers have had the same problem in trying to ascertain Aristophanes' views on politics or such social issues as gender relations. Do his attacks on Cleon indicate that he was "conservative"? Do his so-called peace-plays (*The Acharnians, Peace, Lysistrata*), which clearly articulated a longing for the end of the Peloponnesian War (a conflict between Athens and Sparta that lasted for nearly three decades, from 431 to 404), indicate the poet's disapproval of current Athenian war policy? Do the cluster of plays that highlight women (*Lysistrata, Celebrating Ladies, The Sexual Congress*) reveal the poet to be anachronistically enlightened about women—a protofeminist? The plays can easily suggest such conclusions, but in fact no really systematic political or social outlook is forthcoming from them. Characters will take apparently clear political stands at one moment in a play, only to undermine them elsewhere, usually for the sake of a good laugh. And when it comes to Aristophanes' sexual politics we must remain agnostic as to whether the power and status he affords women in some of his plots were received as a prescription for social change—or as an extended joke "among the guys" who made up most of the audience.

Rather than dwell on Aristophanes' personal beliefs, which we can never hope to recover anyway, let us focus on the politics and poetics of comic satire as a literary genre. In line with the antagonistic dynamic of such poetry and the poet's need to find in his surroundings something worthy of mockery, something that would strike a chord in an audience that was pitting his comic sensibility against that of his rivals, Aristophanes naturally gravitates to topics that generate controversy in nearly all societies: domestic and international politics, celebrity lives and their scandals, popular entertainment, education, and so forth. These are areas in which the slightest eccentricity can seem amusing, especially when exaggerated by caricature and incongruity. Any deviation from "the way things were" is always fodder for a satirist, and Aristophanes is famous for plots that dramatize the conflict between the "traditional old" and the "unconventional new," whether these dramatize old and new generations (e.g., *Clouds*, *Wasps*), political ideologies (e.g., *The Suits*, *The Sexual Congress*), or poetic styles (e.g., *Celebrating Ladies*, *Frogs*). This explains the general conservative feeling of so many of the plays, an almost wistful yearning for life to remain stable and ordered when the progress of time inevitably ensures that it cannot. It also explains why politicians then in office, for example, or philosopher-professors teaching for pay, were natural targets of comic ridicule: they existed in the here-and-now, and they had the potential to influence everyone's life. Any false step of theirs could cause intense anxiety within the demos, and one way the Athenians grappled with this anxiety was to reprocess it as comic performance. Comedy probably did little to change whatever views on political and moral issues audiences brought with them to the theater (it might seem remarkable, for instance, that not long after Aristophanes' unrelieved attack on Cleon in *The Suits* won first prize, the Athenians elected Cleon general), but comic poetry would certainly have encouraged them to refine their perspectives on the complex ideological forces that governed their city and their own interpersonal behavior.

As a form of public art, organized and at least partially funded by the state, Old Comedy necessarily reflected prevailing cultural norms, and its success depended largely on its ability to walk the fine line between questioning—and occasionally subverting—these norms and merely endorsing them. The generally conservative tendencies of satire were no doubt ultimately reassuring to a democracy that institutionalized the comic performances to begin with. One cannot easily imagine, after all, what group would endorse an art form that seriously repudiated its fundamental claims to legitimacy, and few looking back today on the audience of Aristophanes' time would deny that Aristophanic comedy presupposes the desirability of democracy as practiced in the fifth century. Certainly the ancient testimony mentioned earlier, even if fictional, that Cleon sued Aristophanes for slandering the demos and its politicians in his *Babylonians* of 426 suggests that there were perceived limits to comic ridicule at the time. But so far as we can tell these limits were never systematically articulated or, for that matter, rigorously enforced. It was probably less the fear of any slander laws that restricted the freedom of comic poets than a finely honed sense of what the audience—the demos itself—would find humorous.

Although we possess only eleven complete plays by Aristophanes (representing perhaps a quarter of his total output), we are fortunate that these eleven offer examples of his art from every period of his career. Readers who approach them chronologically will note that the latest plays, both from the fourth century, *The Sexual Congress* (392) and *Wealth* (388), reflect changes in structure and content from those composed in the fifth century. The most conspicuous difference lies in the diminishing role of the chorus. In its earliest stages comedy, like tragedy, was as much a spectacle of music and dance as of spoken verse, and the chorus was clearly an area in which costume, song, and gesture could be combined to create a theatrical extravaganza. Eight of Aristophanes' surviving plays, in fact, take their titles from the identity of the chorus, and in all of the fifth-century plays his choruses play an integral role in the plot (*Frogs* is a quirky exception in that it has two choruses—the frogs themselves and a band of religious initiates; the frogs appear only briefly, at the beginning, and the initiates take over the choral duties for the rest of the play). *The Sexual Congress* and *Wealth* still have choruses, but their role is, by contrast, highly restricted and at times almost obtrusive. Some of the manuscripts of these plays indicate places in the text where someone (the poet, perhaps, but we cannot be sure) was expected to add a choral song and dance as a kind of interlude. Some scholars have even suggested that these were points in the play where the chorus was expected to improvise ad libitum while the actors prepared for the next scene. The details remain uncertain, but we can say with confidence that song and dance were increasingly relegated to the sidelines, used as ornamentation and framing, but no longer deemed necessary for the advancement of the plot.

Two other changes in Aristophanes' fourth-century plays throw into relief the process by which Old Comedy gradually developed into its later forms, Middle and New Comedy. First, the parabasis all but disappeared by the fourth century, and as a result, the poet's carefully constructed relationship with his audience became necessarily less explicit. Second, even though the non-Aristophanic examples of Middle Comedy are fragmentary, it seems clear that the pointed satire, the personal, often obscene abuse we associate with Old Comedy was significantly softened. Both these changes are in keeping with a general fourth-century trend away from strictly topical, highly episodic plots, such as we find in Old Comedy, toward plots that display greater narrative coherence and linearity. Earlier concerns with specific events and personalities of the day slowly gave way to "universalizing" topics of human interest, which can be vividly seen in the popularity of stock comic characters—cooks, slaves, philosophers, misers, misanthropes, and so forth.

The shifts in public taste that Middle and New Comedy reflect are not easy to account for, but doubtless the dissolution of the Athenian empire after the Peloponnesian War and an internationalizing movement of culture in the fourth century are at least partly responsible. Were our evidence better for the period, we would probably find that the development of Greek comic drama, as well as its public reception, was hardly as uniform as we tend to construe it. Compare in this regard the state of comic drama in our own culture. Aristophanes' rambunctious, topical satire is reincarnated in late-night talk-shows, British series such as *Benny Hill* or *Fawlty Towers*, Gilbert and Sullivan revivals, Marx Brothers movies, and Three Stooges shorts. Yet at the same time, contemporary popular taste seems generally to favor the genres that look more like Middle or New Comedy, as is clear from the fact that the situation comedy has held sway on television for several decades. No doubt the Greeks of both the fifth and fourth centuries also had the capacity to appreciate a variety of comic styles, and poets could be found to cater to all tastes. We have only scattered remnants of such poets, and only a skeletal understanding of how comedy evolved, but the literary eclecticism that Aristophanes alone displays across his entire career testifies to a poetic catholicity that would be remarkable in any age.

The Suits

Translated by
Greg Delanty

Translator's Preface

During the 1970s the Regime of the Colonels in Greece banned performance of all Aristophanes' plays. This fact suggests how subversive these works still are, and perhaps no other play of Aristophanes is more subversive than *The Suits*, originally called *The Knights*. All the plays of Aristophanes derive from the people and events of his time. *The New Class* is a satiric attack on Cleon, the Athenian demagogue, his political and military policy, and the public who voted him into power.

The play was first performed at the Lenaea in 424 B.C., and won for Aristophanes first prize over his fellow playwrights Cratinus (whom he ridicules in this play) and Aristomenes. Because of his signal victory the previous summer at Sphacteria during the Peloponnesian War, the majority of Athenians saw Cleon as a hero. He had been given every possible privilege and, early in 424, seemed certain to be elected as one of the generals for the coming year. It was at this point that Aristophanes' play was performed.

The satire is scornful and pessimistic throughout. The Athenian public is represented by the bumbling, vain, stupid, lazy, and extremely malleable figure of Demos (literally, in Greek, "the People"). Toward the conclusion of the play Demos relates that he is dimwitted on purpose in order to fool those who, he says, are under the illusion that they are fooling him:

> . . . I'm only letting on that I'm an easy ride. I get such pleasure
>> each day taking all this in. I purposely set up a scoundrel
>> to be my prime minister. Then, when the time is ripe
>> and he's as big as he can get, I'll screw him. (613)

Demos' "I'm no fool" attitude, however, does not hold water, for he is hoodwinked and abused throughout the play. He has been ruled by a tyrant, a tanner—and this tanner is ousted by a sausage seller who is an even more cunning scoundrel.

The Suits rings as true today as no doubt it did when first staged, but to retain that pointedness I have made alterations to bring it into the present day, even while remaining as faithful as possible to the original spirit. For instance, my version of the title helps make contemporary connections. In Aristophanes' day, the upwardly mobile class of entrepreneurs was called the "hippeis," meaning "horsemen" or, as often rendered, "knights." To avoid the distracting and irrelevant association with medieval warriors in chain mail, I have renamed the play *The Suits*, which seems the closest equivalent.

Because the speeches of the chorus are occasionally long, for the sake of variety I have divided the actual chorus into three distinct parts. When Demosthenes is crying for help from the suits early in the play, he specifically asks for two members, Simon and Panaetius, thought to be the real names of two leaders of the Athenian cavalry. They also speak substantial parts individually, even though they are not mentioned in the original text after Demosthenes cries for help. These two characters, for the most part, speak in prose, which to my mind is more in keeping with the down-to-earth quality of the main characters. The chorus as a whole, however, generally speaks in verse, especially when the action is heightened and intense—the other characters of the play speak in verse when the drama warrants it. An adventurous director might have at least a few verse sections of the chorus sung as if on Broadway. There is controversy as to whether the chorus initially rides in on real horses or on something like hobbyhorses, which might be more effective, even hobbyhorses all with the head of Paphlagon.

Indeed, a director could easily take the demagogic liberty of contemporizing the play in a way appropriate to the time and place of the production. For instance, an American director today could change the names of the demagogic tanner and sausage seller who vie for power throughout the play from Paphlagon and Agoracritus to Paphragon and Agoraclintonus, and those of characters like Simon and Panaetius to Simonopolous and Panopolous. The production might have the chorus ski onto the stage waving the U.S. flag and carrying "Down with Paphlagon" slogans. Contemporizing the names of certain characters with such bogus-sounding Greek names along with the insertion of other present-day allusions should give contemporary audiences reason to laugh as audiences must have when the play was originally staged. This treatment would be true to the comedy of Aristophanes, whose characters were simply masks of contemporary people and whose references and puns are sometimes lost on us.

From the play it is clear that the two other main characters, Demosthenes and Nicias, are caricatures of real generals in the Athenian army. Demosthenes was a rival to Cleon and believed by some to have been more responsible than Cleon for the Athenian victory at Pylos. The sidekick of Demosthenes, Nicias, true to record, is portrayed as a more wimpish, overly careful, and fearful character.

The Suits, unrestrained by the conventions of tragedy, is more open, free-flowing, ordinary, and thus more akin to the drama of today. This play could be performed in a kind of burlesque fashion with popular music. One could conceive of Mel Brooks producing it. The slapstick entry of Demosthenes and Nicias at the beginning reminds me of the brace of Beckettian characters, Vladimir and Estragon, in *Waiting for Godot*. In keeping with modern-day comedy, it is worth noting that a certain amount of the bawdiness is fixated on behinds and bowel systems, prefiguring the Freudian theories of the anality of those obsessed with money and power.

It is curious that Aristophanes got away with the satiric attack at every level on the Athenians and on Cleon himself. All the actors wore representative masks—a convention that, by the way, would make it easy for a director today to refer to a modern-day cast of characters. Aristophanes actually played the part of Paphlagon (Cleon), and this, perhaps, allowed him to say whatever he wished, for Cleon may have thought that to have Aristophanes play him was a kind of inverted compliment. He may even have enjoyed it in the same way Ronald Reagan or Bill Clinton enjoys the mockery of the likes of Johnny Carson or Jay Leno. *The Suits* was the first play that Aristophanes produced himself, and this also may have been a factor in its popular success. The parabasis, the intermission of action in which the chorus addresses the audience directly in song or recitative, introduces him to the audience:

> Ladies and gentlemen, it's chorus time, and we admit—
> since you're all such aficionados of comedy and wit—
> that had any comic playwright of the old days
> begged us to take part in one of his plays,

it's dubious, frankly, he'd have had a chance.
But this chap, Aristophanes, shares our stance.
He speaks right up and doesn't try to dupe
the truth, even if it'll land him in the soup.
Aristophanes. Have you never heard of his name?
You look cagey. You're wondering what's his game. (264–73)

Perhaps the boldness of the parabasis explains how Aristophanes managed to get away with such effrontery directed at Cleon, his followers, and even the public at large.

I hope, should any present-day tanners and sausage sellers ever see my version performed, that they take their cue from the reactions of Cleon and Athenian audiences. Still, who knows? The regime of the Colonels may storm the theater and ban this play once more.

I wish to thank Katharine Washburn for her help with this translation.

Cast

*(In front of Demos' house in Athens. There is a general hubbub from
inside, and Demosthenes and Nicias are flung out through the
door by Paphlagon's bouncers. Their worse-for-wear uniforms
indicate that they once held high positions.)*

DEMOSTHENES

    Ouch! Oh! We're in the shit now. That bastard. That slimy, ass-
            licking Paphlagon. May the gods give him a taste
            of his own medicine, him and his shenanigans.
            Ever since he got here he's been a pain in the
            ass. He's nothing but trouble. He's done a
            number on us.

NICIAS

    You said it, brother. May that bad-mouthing Paphlagon get his
            comeuppance.

DEMOSTHENES

    Relax. Take it easy. How are you doing?

NICIAS
 Lousy, like yourself.

DEMOSTHENES
 Come here, old pal. Let's croon a duet. You know that number
  one tearjerker.
(They raise a dreadful duet of meaningless words from some pop song.)

BOTH
 Oh Boo Boo Boo . . . O U U U . . . Oh Boo Boo Boo Boo . . .

DEMOSTHENES
 Fuck it. Enough of all this bitching and feeling sorry for
  ourselves. We should try to figure a way out
  of this.

NICIAS
 Is there a way?

DEMOSTHENES
 You tell me.

NICIAS
 I'm not good at stuff like that. It's your bright idea. You spout it
  out. I'm no fancy-pants Euripides. I'm no smart-
  ass, tidy tragedian: "Could you but spout for me
  what I must spout."   10

DEMOSTHENES
 You must think I'm green. Don't sell me that crock. Sprout some
  other caper.

NICIAS
 Okeydoke. Say after me then . . . Lettuce, beet . . .

DEMOSTHENES
 Lettuce, beet . . .

NICIAS
Now add the word "it" . . .

DEMOSTHENES
"It"?

NICIAS
Yes. You're on the ball. Now imagine that you are actually playing
with your sausage and jerk off with the words.
You know how you speed up the more you pull
the baldy man with one eye. Say: Let us, beat it . . .

NICIAS
Lettuce, beet, it . . . Lettuce beet it . . . Letusbeetit . . .
Let'sbeatit . . . let'sbeatit . . .

NICIAS
Well, doesn't that feel good?

DEMOSTHENES
Fucking fabulous, but I'm a bit wary of playing with myself.

NICIAS
What?   20

DEMOSTHENES
Because they say that choking the old turkey makes you bald as a
turkey.

NICIAS
God, there is only one thing for it so. We'll have to get down on
our knees and pray.

DEMOSTHENES
Now honestly, do you really believe there are gods?

NICIAS
I sure do.

DEMOSTHENES
How do you know?

NICIAS
Because the gods dumped all this crap on us.

DEMOSTHENES
A sound answer, but enough of that. Let's explain to the audience how we got up to our necks in shit.

NICIAS
A good idea. But first let's find out if they're on our side.

DEMOSTHENES *(to audience)*
Listen, now. We have a cranky, green bean of a master called Demos, short for democracy or, in his case, Demuck, or is it Demockcrazy? A month ago this geezer bought a slave who's a tanner named Paphlagon. He's a shifty, scandal-mongering bastard.
This shyster had the old man copped immediately. He's an actor if ever there was one. He fell at our master's feet and licked ass. He tricked and wheedled Demos with bits of old leather, saying stuff like "Demos, take it easy. One case is enough to have to judge. Come home and I'll run a soothing bath for your poor, overworked body," or "Here take a drop of this," or "Swallow that," or "Here are three obols."   30
Paphlagon grabs anything we prepare and makes a gift of it to our master. Only the other day I baked a scrumptious cake at Pylos, but your man snatched it as soon as my back was turned and presented it to dumb Demos. He stymies us every time. He's always there hovering around the table waiting to swat us off like flies.

Old Demos is hooked on the oracles. Demos is especially gone
          on that prophetess Sibyl, and Paphlagon reads
          him her half-baked whoreoscopes. Paphlagon
          has realized that our master is gullible. He feeds
          him false accusations about everyone. We get
          scourged while that operator hounds the servants
          and makes a killing.
He frightens the life out of us all with threats like "Look at how
          Hylas is flogged by my orders. If you don't do
          what I want, you'll get the same treatment." So
          we are forced to kowtow and cough up.

(to Nicias)

    Now, old buddy, let's figure out what the best thing to do is and
          who'll help us.

NICIAS

    The only reliable way is "the lettuce beet it" recipe.

DEMOSTHENES

    But how can we when Paphlagon has eyes everywhere? He
          straddles the whole damn place, with one leg
          in Pylos and the other in the assembly. His hole
          squats over Chaosmos, his arms are on
          Extortionia, and his head over Larcenia.

NICIAS

    There's only one safe place for us, and that's six feet under.

DEMOSTHENES

    Yes, but it has to be an honorable death.

NICIAS

    Now what could be the most manly? Maybe we could take
          poison like Themistocles. He knocked back
          a gallon of bull's blood instead of giving in
          to the king.

DEMOSTHENES

> Fuck that. The best way out is not to guzzle bull's blood, but
> wine, the nectar of the gods. Maybe the god
> of booze will come up with some idea.   40

NICIAS

> Drink. Drink. That's all you ever think about. How can a guy
> think straight with drink taken?

DEMOSTHENES

> What? Have you water on the brain? You need a proper drink to
> straighten you out. Are you stupid enough to piss
> on the fountain of inspiration? Can't you see that
> when guys drink they're merry, congenial, and
> overflowing with courage? I'll show you. Pass me
> that flagon and I'll prove what a great inspiration
> wine can be.

NICIAS

> Getting tanked won't solve anything.

DEMOSTHENES

> That's what you think. Fetch the wine.
> *(Nicias goes inside, cursing.)*
> I'll settle down here and prepare myself to spout great thoughts
> and plans.
> *(He reclines on the ground in a grand fashion as if in a symposium.*
> *Nicias returns, grumbling, with the wine.)*

NICIAS

> You can't imagine how lucky you are that I managed to pinch
> this.

DEMOSTHENES

> What's Paphlagon up to?

NICIAS

    The bastard has just devoured the confiscated pickled cakes, and
        now he's out for the count.

DEMOSTHENES

    Serves him right. Now fill me up.

NICIAS

    Cheers. Here's to your good spirits.   50

DEMOSTHENES

    Here's to the spirit of liquor.
(He drinks and muses.)
    Spirit of spirits, I knew you'd come up with the answer.

NICIAS

    What is it? What is it?

DEMOSTHENES

    Sneak inside while Paphlagon is snoozing and pinch the oracles.

NICIAS

    Whatever you say, but I've a feeling that your good spirit will
        come back to haunt me.
(He goes inside.)

DEMOSTHENES

    One more won't do me any harm. It'll irrigate the old brain cells
        and maybe I'll spout a bright idea or two.
(He drinks; Nicias returns with a scroll.)

NICIAS

    Paphlagon is farting and sawing wood so much that he didn't
        catch me knocking off his sacred oracle, the one
        he guards so carefully.

DEMOSTHENES
>Good man, yourself. Let me pore over it while you pour me
>>another.
(He opens the scroll.)
>Now what does it say? Pass me the wine, pronto.

NICIAS
>Here you go. Now what does it say?   60

DEMOSTHENES *(raising the cup he has just emptied)*
>Fill this dead man up again.

NICIAS
>That's the oracle, "Fill this dead man up again"?

DEMOSTHENES
>O glorious booze.

NICIAS
>Come on. What's the story?

DEMOSTHENES
>Quick. Pour me another.

NICIAS *(handing Demosthenes a refilled cup)*
>This Bakis is surely under the table by now.

DEMOSTHENES
>Oh, that blackguard Paphlagon! So that's why he was so careful
>>about not letting anyone see. This scared the shit
>>out of him.

NICIAS
>Huh?

DEMOSTHENES
>It forecasts his downfall.

NICIAS

    How?

DEMOSTHENES

    Well, the oracle says, in its own way, how the first to be roped in
            to lead the city is a rope seller.

NICIAS

    That's one huckster. Now what comes next?

DEMOSTHENES

    The next ruler is a sheep dealer.

NICIAS

    That makes two hucksters. Now what's on the cards for him?

DEMOSTHENES

    To boss us all around until another cadging codger, worse
            even than himself, beats the hide off him.
            Paphlagon, that cowboy, steals his way into the
            fold and then lets an almighty torrent out of him.

NICIAS

    Are you saying that the leather man is to be overcome by the
            cowboy?

DEMOSTHENES

    Bulls-eye!

NICIAS

    Holy cow! If only some other cowboy would turn up.

DEMOSTHENES

    We have one hope, a man who has the right trade.

NICIAS
Come on . . . Who is this guy?   80

DEMOSTHENES
Take a guess.

NICIAS
Oh, come on. I haven't an iota.

DEMOSTHENES
The guy who'll give Paphlagon the boot is a sausage monger.

NICIAS
A sauce-sage man. By god, what a swell trade. But where is this
            guy?

DEMOSTHENES
Let's keep an eye out for him.
(A sausage seller approaches, pushing his stall.)

NICIAS
Well, thank our lucky stars, here's our man.

DEMOSTHENES
Saw-sage man, please come here. You are our savior. Come on,
            tell us who you really are.

SAUSAGE SELLER
What? What do you want? What's your beef?

DEMOSTHENES
Join us here. I want to tell you of your good fortune.

NICIAS
Take his tray and tell him about the oracle while I go and look
            for Paphlagon.   90
(He goes into the house.)

DEMOSTHENES

Firstly, put down all your stuff and give the earth and the gods
their due.

SAUSAGE SELLER

Okay.
(He's somewhat puzzled, but does as he's told.)
But, now, what's all this about?

DEMOSTHENES

You are the luckiest man alive. From sausages to sovereignty.
You're to become the boss of Athens.

SAUSAGE SELLER

Give me a break. Quit all this tripe. Let me get on about my
business.

DEMOSTHENES

What tripe? Tripe? Do you call them tripe?
(points to the audience)
Look at them, stacked one behind the other.

SAUSAGE SELLER

Okay. Okay.

DEMOSTHENES

You're the top dog over the whole kit and caboodle, over the
market, banks, ass-embly. It's all yours. You can
tramp over the council and curtail the generals.
You can toss them in prison and get your oats
courtesy of the taxpayer.

SAUSAGE SELLER

You can't be serious?

DEMOSTHENES

> I've never been more serious. You ain't seen nothing yet. Take a
> gander at all the islands around.   100

SAUSAGE SELLER

> Okay. So what?

DEMOSTHENES

> What do you mean, "So what"? Are you blind? Can't you see all
> those trading posts?

SAUSAGE SELLER

> Sure, but . . .

DEMOSTHENES

> Well, is there anyone luckier than you? And on top of this, take a
> look at Caria and then Carthage.

SAUSAGE SELLER

> Shit, what's the good of all this gaping? I'm going cock-eyed.

DEMOSTHENES

> Cock-eyed or no, it's all yours. You can do anything you want
> with it. The oracle declares that you're going
> to be cock of the walk over the whole shebang.
> You're going to be a great man.

SAUSAGE SELLER

> You're pulling my leg. Explain to me how I, a mere sausage man,
> am going to become such a big deal.

DEMOSTHENES

> Can't you see, this is precisely the reason why you will be a big
> man. You are a crafty, low-down dealer who will
> stoop to anything to get what you want.

SAUSAGE SELLER
    Now honestly, you're embarrassing me. I could never consider
            myself to be as big as all that.

DEMOSTHENES
    Bull! It's out of character for you to declare you are not the right
            man for the job? Could there be something good
            about you? What a bummer, a flawed character.
            You don't come from law-abiding stock, heaven
            forbid, or anything like that, do you?   110

SAUSAGE SELLER
    Heavens, no—I come from nothing but bad blood.

DEMOSTHENES
    Thank heaven. Put it there.
    (They shake hands.)
    We couldn't be luckier. You're a born politician.

SAUSAGE SELLER
    But, my friend, I have no education, except for a bit of reading
            and writing.

DEMOSTHENES
    That you've got any at all is more the pity. The last thing a leader
            of the people needs to be is an educated man or a
            good guy. What's needed is an ignorant wheeler-
            dealer. Don't miss this opportunity.

SAUSAGE SELLER
    All right, all right. But what does the oracle really say anyway?

DEMOSTHENES
    Here, take a gawk. By god, it bodes well. The oracle is full of
            fairly high-falutin', symbolic lingo. Listen:

When the leathery, crooked-clawed eagle
swoops down on the bloody snake in the grass,
then Paphlagon will be in a right pickle   120
and he's sure to end up on his ass—
that's if, of course, the right type
of man is willing to give up his tripe.

SAUSAGE SELLER
    So? Where do I fit in to all this?

DEMOSTHENES
    Well, of course, the eagle of leathery hide is obviously Paphlagon.

SAUSAGE SELLER
    But what about that crooked bit?

DEMOSTHENES
    That's obvious. It speaks for itself. Think about it. He's crooked
                and flies about snatching everything for himself.

SAUSAGE SELLER
    And what's this snake baloney about?

DEMOSTHENES
    Now come on. Are you blind or what? Snakes are long and
                slippery, and so are sausages. They are slimy and
                full of blood. That implies that the snake in the
                grass is about to bring down the leathery eagle.
                But he must catch on to this and snatch his
                chance.

SAUSAGE SELLER
    All this is making me dizzy. I'm puzzled by the thought that I'm
                supposed to be able to rule the people. That's
                wacky.   130

DEMOSTHENES

Wacky, my ass. Nothing could be simpler. You just have to go
on plying your trade as usual. Stir up the stew.
Make a right hash of it. And if you think it needs
sweetening, then pour on the sugary words. You
have everything else a tyrant needs with your
loud-mouthed harangue, your base background
and guttersnipe ways. You have the perfect
character for politics, and the oracle backs this.
Come on now, raise a mug to the god of nincompoops, dopes,
fools, assholes, cowboys—and then let's see you
shear Paphlagon's hide.

SAUSAGE SELLER

But who's going to take my side? The well-heeled are scared
shitless of him and the down-at-heel shit in their
trousers at the mention of his name.

DEMOSTHENES

Haven't you got the best class on your side? The suits? They're the
knights of society—the whole lot of them. They
are the up-and-coming class. And along with this
classy class you have honest, good citizens among
the rabble who back you. Last but not least,
ourselves and the gods. Don't wet your pants.
You won't be able to recognize the dictator by his features, since
no one has dared to make a mask of him or
portray him. Nonetheless, people aren't stupid;
they'll know him when they see him.

NICIAS *(from within)*

Oh shit, here comes Paphlagon. Heaven help us.

PAPHLAGON *(rushing out of the house)*

By heaven, you haven't a prayer. You'll never pull this off.
(He knocks over the wine cup.)

What's this? The conspirator's concoction? Coupzou? So you are
        drinking to a coup. Do you think I'm stupid?
        Don't budge. You've had it.
(The sausage seller turns to escape.)

DEMOSTHENES *(to the sausage seller)*
    Hey, hey, where are you hightailing it to? Hold your ground.
        Don't let the cause down now. You are our hope,
        our savior, our sausage seller. Don't skedaddle
        out of here and leave us in the stew.
(shouting off stage)
    Give us the suits; give us the knights! Now's your time. Simon
        and Panaetius, come on.   140
(to the sausage seller)
    They're on their way. Turn back and make your stand. Look at
        the dust their horses kick up.
(pointing to Paphlagon)
    Take him on now. Give him his just deserts and chase him off.
        Give him the ol' hi-de-ho.
(The sausage seller makes sure the suits are coming and then turns back.
        He and Demosthenes face Paphlagon as the chorus
        of suits charge in. They are all riding hobbyhorses
        with the face of Paphlagon.)

SIMON
    Beat him. Horsewhip the whelp, the bounder who has upset
        our cavalry. He'd steal the eyes out of your head
        if you weren't looking. Thief, thief, thief. We
        cannot say the word too often, since he's a villain
        umpteen times a day. Whip him, whack him,
        smack him. Give the scoundrel a right roasting.
        Show him how much we can't stand him. Let's
        roar him down.
    But watch him. This piece of shit knows how Eucrates slipped
        out so easily, as easily as crap slips out after bran.

PAPHLAGON

Gentlemen, gentlemen. Brothers of justice, I supported you with
my fast-talking act whether you were right or
wrong. Help me now. I'm beset by conspirators.

PANAETIUS

That is correct. You squander the public funds that belong to us
all. You devour the ministers of finance as if they
are figs, squeezing them to see which of them is
still green, which ripe, and which gone to seed.
On top of that, you're talented at picking the
green ones who're shaky on the branch, the ones
who are vulnerable in the pecking order. You
skin, squash, and suck them dry.

PAPHLAGON

What? Don't tell me that you're behind them—and just after I've
proposed a monument in honor of you.

SIMON

Bullshit. We weren't born yesterday. He never gives up, does he?
Look how he's trying to brown nose us. He must
take us for assholes. But all his trickery will
finally rebound on him, and no matter what way
he ducks and dives we'll trip him up.

PAPHLAGON *(to the audience)*

Citizens, friends, look how they're hitting me below the belt.

SAUSAGE SELLER

What pandemonium. You make the same old hullabaloo every
time, upsetting the city.　　　　150

PAPHLAGON

It's the same row that'll send you running with your tail between
your legs.

PANAETIUS
>Ok, then, if you can outbawl him, then you can have the cake.
>>But if you don't, then we'll take it and eat it too.

PAPHLAGON *(pointing to the sausage seller)*
>I denounce this imposter. I know his type. He shipped contra
>>sausages and blood pudding to the enemy.

SAUSAGE SELLER
>Two can play at that game. By god, I denounce you. You rush
>>into the great hall with an empty belly and you
>>stroll out full to the gills.

DEMOSTHENES
>By god, that's not a lie. He lifts bread, meat, and fish in broad
>>daylight. Not even Pericles could do that.

PAPHLAGON
>You two have had it. Kaput!

SAUSAGE SELLER
>Paphlagon, you're all bluster. I can holler three times as loud
>>as you.

PAPHLAGON
>I'll drown you out with my roar.

SAUSAGE SELLER
>I'll sink you with mine before you can.

PAPHLAGON
>If you become the general I'll blacken your name. You know
>>what happens when you give a dog a bad name.   160

SAUSAGE SELLER
>I'll bark back at you like a mad dog.

PAPHLAGON
> I'll make you whimper like a frightened pup.

SAUSAGE SELLER
> I'll bring you to heel.

PAPHLAGON
> Do you dare to look at me straight in the eye?

SAUSAGE SELLER
> I was brought up a cur, too, a mongrel from the market place.

PAPHLAGON
> I'll eat you alive if you let a grunt out of you.

SAUSAGE SELLER
> If you open your mouth you'll end up dog shit.

PAPHLAGON
> I swear I'm the real cur, the real swindler. You pale next to me.

SAUSAGE SELLER
> Are you joking? Of course I'm a swindler. I can rob the eyes out
> of your head when you aren't looking and then,
> when you are, I'll swear I haven't pinched them.

PAPHLAGON
> You're such a liar. On top of everything, I'll expose you for not
> paying taxes on your sacred tripe.   170

SIMON
> Whelp, pup, big mouth. You have some neck, some cheek.
> You've polluted all of Athens. You've wreaked
> havoc on the whole community. You've drowned
> everyone else out and hover above the rising
> tributaries of the city, waiting to catch every
> passing fish.

PAPHLAGON
> I know the leather that you have sewn this conspiracy with.

SAUSAGE SELLER
> Sure you do. If you don't know your own leather stitching, then
> I don't know my sausage making. You cut strips
> of hide from the side so that it looks thicker than
> it really is. You cheat the local yokels into buying
> it, but after two or three days the sandals stretch
> to twice their size.

DEMOSTHENES
> Blast him, didn't he catch me with the same trick. He made a
> laughing stock of me. I was swimming in my
> shoes before I ever reached Pergase.

PANAETIUS *(to Paphlagon)*
> You're a born finagler, conniver, which of course is the one
> essential quality needed to be a true politician.
> You have such balls. You even cut into the purses
> of the well-heeled foreigners who visit here. You
> broke generous Archeptohemus, who showered
> the city with gifts.
> But now, big man, you've met more than your match, and there
> is no one more thrilled than us to know the
> scoundrel that will bring you down. It's as clear
> as day that he can beat you at your own game.
(to the sausage seller)
> Now tell us how a good upbringing isn't worth a bean.

SAUSAGE SELLER
> Now listen to what sort of guy he is.

PAPHLAGON
> Won't you let me speak?

SAUSAGE SELLER
>No way will I let you open your trap. Are you joking? I'm even
>>lower than you.   180

DEMOSTHENES
>And if that doesn't stop him, tell him how all your family before
>>you were the lowest of the low.

PAPHLAGON
>Are you still not going to let me get a word in edgewise?

SAUSAGE SELLER
>Nope!

PAPHLAGON
>By golly, you will or I'll boil over.

SAUSAGE SELLER
>No, I won't.

PANAETIUS
>Let this geezer explode.

PAPHLAGON
>Who do you think you are, anyway, to think that you can talk to
>>me like this?

SAUSAGE SELLER
>Because your delivery is sure to stir things up and make
>>things hot.

PAPHLAGON
>*Delivery*—that's a load of tripe. If some business came your way,
>>you'd certainly know how to make a hash of it.
>>Do you want me to lay it out for you? You think,
>>just because you won some stinking, lousy case

against some outsider, that you can swallow
anyone whole and spit him out.
You probably stayed up all night rehearsing your case, mumbling
it through the streets, bugging everyone you
met, drinking water to clear your throat. You
blatherer, you haven't a notion of what it takes.   190

SAUSAGE SELLER

And what magic potion do you yourself swig that gives you the
one and only power to numb the city and render
everyone dumb?

PAPHLAGON

There's no one to match me. I can devour a whole tuna and
guzzle a full jar of vino and still be able to screw
the generals at Pylos.

PANAETIUS

We are taken by most of what you said, but the one thing that
troubles us is that you seem to intend guzzling all
the political gravy yourself. Will you leave any for
anyone else?

PAPHLAGON *(pointing to the sausage seller)*
He won't devour the Milesians by eating fish.

SAUSAGE SELLER

But I'll eat a side of beef and then get drunk and buy off the great
silver mines.
(to Panaetius and the rest of the chorus)
Gravy, I'll give you gravy. There'll be plenty to go around.

PAPHLAGON

I'll rush to the senate and shake them up.

SAUSAGE SELLER

And I'll make sausages out of your guts.

PAPHLAGON

> Go ahead, make my day. I'll grab you by the ass and fling you out
> the door on your nut.

SIMON

> By heaven, if you take him like that, you'll have to take us first.   200

PAPHLAGON

> I'll tie you up in knots.

SAUSAGE SELLER

> I'll show up your yellow hide.

PAPHLAGON

> I'll stretch your green hide on the rack.

SAUSAGE SELLER

> I'll strip your hide and make a pickpocket's purse out of it.

PAPHLAGON

> I'll pin you down and pull you apart.

SAUSAGE SELLER

> I'll make mincemeat out of you.

PAPHLAGON

> I'll pluck out your eyelashes one by one.

SAUSAGE SELLER

> I'll scalp you.

DEMOSTHENES

> Then we'll shove a fork in his mouth, like a butcher, and rip out
> his tongue. We'll be able to look down his throat
> to see how much of a swine he is.

SIMON

So, we have someone here fierier than fire, whose brazen
speeches outbrazen cheek itself. This is serious.
Grab him and give him the full treatment. Don't
spare him, now that you've got him by the balls.
He's sure to show how much of a yellow belly he
is. We all know what this guy is really like.   210

SAUSAGE SELLER

He's always been like this. It's only by reaping another man's
harvest that he has made his name. And now he
has prisoners tied up like ears of corn. They're
over there drying out before he attempts to
sell them.

PAPHLAGON (*sarcastically*)

I'm so scared of you I'm trembling all over. Look.
(*feigns trembling all over his body*)
Young feller, I can't be touched as long as the council and people
look cluelessly on.

SIMON

Heaven help us, this guy's got no shame. He'll brazen everything
out right to the end. I'd rather be a wet blanket
in Cratinus' piss-soaked sheets, or play a tragedy
by poor Morsimus, than be on his side.

(*to Paphlagon*)

May all the extorted money that you've crammed down your
gullet be spewed back up as easily as you
devoured it. Only then will we raise our voice
and toast, "Drink, drink for this is capital news."
I bet you even miserly Iulius will lift his voice
and cheer·to high heaven.

PAPHLAGON

If you think you'll outdo me, then you've got another think
coming, by god. If you do, I swear that I'll never
again share a morsel of the meat offered up at

public gatherings to none other than Zeus
himself.

SAUSAGE SELLER

And I swear by all the strappings that I got when I was a
        stripling, along with all the cuts I got from
        butchers' knives, that I'd cut the feet from under
        you any day. This is as obvious as my proud
        paunch, rounded by gravy-soaked scraps of
        bread thrown out after dinner.

PAPHLAGON

Eating scraps like a mongrel! You are pathetic. How do you
        expect to face down a dog-faced ape on the
        diet of a cur?

SAUSAGE SELLER

What a big mouth! Bluster is your name and bluster is your
        game. You're all bark and no bite. And I've
        umpteen other tricks that I picked up as a
        whippersnapper. I'd divert the kitchen's attention
        with yelling something like: "Look, the swallows
        are back. It's spring." As soon as the cooks took
        the bait and looked up, I swiped the meat.

SIMON

What a crackerjack guy! That was a cunning piece of work.
        Before the swallows arrived you scoffed the
        winter store.   220

SAUSAGE SELLER

And not one of them had an inkling. I'd stuff the meat in my
        jockstrap and look as if butter wouldn't melt in
        my mouth. One day, a politician caught me and
        declared, "There's no doubt that one day this
        operator will screw us."

SIMON

> And he was right on. It's as clear as day. The fact that you went on lying even after you were caught red-handed with the spoils bursting from your pants, and still you didn't get your knickers in a twist, is proof positive.

PAPHLAGON

> I'll put a halt to your gallop. I'll put a stop to the lot of you. I'll make mincemeat of you all.

SAUSAGE SELLER

> And I'll pack up my wares and sail into the eye of your bluster and laugh you down.

DEMOSTHENES *(pointing to the sausage seller)*

> And if his hold springs a leak, then we'll bail him out.

PAPHLAGON

> By Demeter, you'll not get away with stealing the talents of so many Athenians.

PANAETIUS *(to the sausage seller)*

> Be careful now, trim your sail. Here's a vehement gale about to capsize you.

SAUSAGE SELLER

> I know damn well that you squeezed ten talents out of Potidaea, that poor, one-horse town way out in the boondocks of Thrace.

PAPHLAGON

> So put your money where your mouth is and take this boon of a talent to keep it shut.

SIMON

This bucko won't be able to stop himself from taking it.   230
(to an imaginary crew)
Ease the shroud now, me laddies, the wind is dropping.

PAPHLAGON

I'll bring four cases against you, demanding hundred-talent fines.

SAUSAGE SELLER

I'll bring twenty against you for draft dodging and more than a
thousand for broad daylight robbery.

PAPHLAGON

I'll declare that you are from a line that abused our goddess.

SAUSAGE SELLER

And I'll declare that your grandfather was in cahoots . . .

PAPHLAGON

In cahoots! What? With whom? How dare you.

SAUSAGE SELLER

In cahoots with the wife of that tyrant Pisistratus—Yah, he sure
lived up to his name. He pissed straight on us.

PAPHLAGON

You're some piss-taker all right.

SAUSAGE SELLER

And I suppose your piss is gold and that you crap gold nuggets.

SIMON

Go on, beat the crap out of him.   240

PAPHLAGON *(to the audience)*
> Help, please. Believe me, these piss artists are out to get me and
> > they won't even give you the steam off their piss.

SIMON
> You have him now. He's shitless. Now go in for the kill and whip
> > him with your guts.
> *(The sausage seller lashes Paphlagon with his tripe and cow's tongue.*
> > *Paphlagon is brought to the ground with the*
> > *flaying. Simon addresses the sausage seller.)*

SIMON
> You have some guts. Such brawn. You're the real goods, there's
> > no doubt about it. You've saved us from being
> > stewed. Look, you've slaughtered him with your
> > tongue.
> *(He points to the cow's tongue that the sausage seller used as a whip.)*
> How can we thank you?

PAPHLAGON *(recovering)*
> God, don't think I didn't know of the plot you were hammering
> > together. Setting the wheels in motion.

SIMON
> Watch it. Watch it. He's talking carpentry now, but you can nail
> > him there too.

SAUSAGE SELLER
> Don't worry, I'm well aware how this crafty tool spliced a deal
> > with the enemy.

SIMON
> Look, look, now he hammers the nails in.

SAUSAGE SELLER
> Oh, we know your slippery handiwork. But don't worry, I'll
> > expose your shoddy workmanship to the people
> > here and the whole lot will fall to pieces on you.

SIMON

What a beauty. Forge him now in his own fashion.   250

SAUSAGE SELLER

And don't think I'm not aware that you have other crafty cohorts
up to similar carry-ons. But if you think that any
of these two-faced characters can bribe me with
one of your back-handers you're berserk. I'll
expose your handiwork to the people.

PAPHLAGON

That's what you think. I'm going to dash over this instant to the
city council and spill the curd you've been
churning with the enemy by night.

SAUSAGE SELLER

Oh, come on, tell us, what's the price of forage among our
enemy? You must be making a fortune. Don't
give us that innocent-as-a-lamb look.

PAPHLAGON

Holy cow, I'll make a stinking great cheese out of you yet.
(He storms out.)

SIMON

All right, now's your chance to strut your stuff, to show us what
you're made of. Now you can prove you're the
genuine article, the man who stuffed the goodies
in his drawers. Hurry up now and leg it to the
chambers before that dirty piece of work lands
us all in the soup.

SAUSAGE SELLER

Okay. Okay. Just give me a moment. I've got to get my tripe and
stuff together before I leave them here for you
to mind.
*(He gathers up the meat he whipped Paphlagon with and sets it back on
his cart.)*

DEMOSTHENES *(handing the sausage seller drippings)*
    Here, grease yourself with this so you can slip his hold.

SAUSAGE SELLER
    Right on. You're no fool, that's certain.

DEMOSTHENES *(offering mustard)*
    Here's something else. Take a dose of this before you go.

SAUSAGE SELLER
    What for?   260

DEMOSTHENES
    So you can get a head start with a fiery argument. Hurry now.
        Get going.

SAUSAGE SELLER
    Relax. Relax. I'm going as fast as I can.

SIMON *(as Demosthenes and the sausage seller go)*
    Now remember, no holds barred. Devour him, boot him, head
            butt him, kick him in the goolies, tear him
            asunder like a mad dog. Bring him down to
            size and come back to us as top dog.
(The chorus begins to dance in a circle.)

    Strophe

    Ladies and gentlemen, it's chorus time, and we admit—
    since you're all such aficionados of comedy and wit—
    that had any comic playwright of the old days
    begged us to take part in one of his plays,
    it's dubious, frankly, he'd have had a chance.
    But this chap, Aristophanes, shares our stance.
    He speaks right up and doesn't try to dupe   270
    the truth, even if it'll land him in the soup.
    Aristophanes. Have you never heard of his name?

You look cagey. You're wondering what's his game.
Why has he hidden in the wings for so long?
He's asked us to explain how, all along,
he has purposely stayed out of the public eye
since he knows comedy is, without a word of a lie,
the toughest of all the arts to pull off.
And he knows also, now don't laugh or cough,
that the taste of the audience can grow quickly cold.   280
You've dumped playwrights as soon as they've grown old.
Look at poor Magnes. He was your favorite,
but as soon as his hair grayed, he didn't rate.
He won all the competitions of his day.
He performed and acted the flute for you in every way,
playing the birds, the Lydians, the mosquitos, even a frog.
But from the day he lost it, you treated him like a dog.
And what about poor, misfortunate Cratinus.
He swept the country with success after success.

Antistrophe

His were the only ditties heard at any sing-along.   290
Staves like "Stupendous Composers of Great Song"
or "Toro, the Thief, Who Didn't Give a Fig."
But these days you won't give him a lousy gig.
Now that his voice is kaput and his harp out of tune,
you don't give a damn. You won't grant him a boon.
He wanders about, mindless from booze, like Connas
wearing his pathetic, bedraggled garland prize.
He's so far gone that he'd drink out of a dirty boot,
while to honor him—even now you don't give a hoot—
he should be given a seat high up in the gods,   300
along with all the flashy politicians and their broads.
And what about Crates, our sorry, old comic?
He concocted his own subtle word-tonic.
And even if at time he was somewhat off,
it was a bit harsh of you, perhaps, to scoff.
So, surely you can understand the predicament

of Aristophanes, wisely wary of such treatment.
Besides, he believes one should know one's craft,
from the bow's jib to the helm's aft,
before setting out on the treacherous ocean.   310
Honestly, don't you think such precaution
is laudable? He didn't sail in here all swagger,
with him perched at the stern, another blasted bragger.
So now come on, raise a wave of applause his way.
Assure this unknown poet he can find haven in this bay.

Epode

Poseidon, god of horses
delighting in their tittuping,
in their excited whinnying,
along with the sleek galleys
rowing over the dark seas   320
and the somersaulting porpoises—
God of gods, son of Cronus,
sacred to these parts,
closest of all to our hearts,
come down today. Be with us.
*(The chorus stops dancing. Each of the following should be said by a
different member of the chorus.)*
Let's salute our ancestors' glory:

They were indomitable on land and sea.

They were always a credit to the country.

They never even blinked an eye at the sight
of the enemy; perpetually ready to fight.   330

And if any of them bit the dust,
they rose, shook themselves and went for bust.

They didn't give a damn about reward
or being honored, not like today's crowd,
who wouldn't lift a finger without pay.

No, that was definitely not their way.

Nor is it ours. We ask for damn all,

Except, maybe, if the enemy should fall,
that we'd get a good scrub-down
and each be allowed to wear a crown.   340

PANAETIUS
    Pallas, keeper of the city,
    goddess of this most sacred country
    with its awesome military,
    not to speak of poetry's standing army,
    come to our aid. Bring us victory
    here today. Trounce our enemy.

SIMON
    And we must not forget our trusty steeds.
    We will praise all their brave deeds,
    but especially extraordinary was the day
    they jumped into our boats in the bay   350
    and with the men they took the oars
    braying, "Gee up now. Gee up." They leaped ashore
    at Corinth, and then each young steed
    sauntered off to find some feed.
    Instead of oats and hay, they had crab.
    They ate so many that a hermit was heard to crab,
    "Poseidon, it's a crying shame that our number's up,
    whether we hide on the beach or in the deep."
(The dance begins again as the sausage seller returns.)

CHORUS
    Welcome back. What a brick.
    We've been worried sick.   360
    Man, your some tough cookie.
    Did you best Tricky Dick?
    Tell us the story quick?

SAUSAGE SELLER
  Sure. Sure. No problem. I whacked him.

CHORUS *(surrounding him and dancing)*
  Well now, three cheers.
  You are some bucko.
  You've spoken well before,
  but please, we're mad to know
  what you said. You've nothing to hide.
  We are all on your side.   370

SAUSAGE SELLER
  Well, wait till you hear this. You'll get a kick out of it. As you
              know, I legged it to the ass-embly and got there
              right on his heels. He was already up to his
              tricks, blowing up a storm of lies about us all.
              Mr. Ass-licking Innocent, himself. The whole
              ass-embly was agog and aghast. He smeared the
              mustard on thick.
  When I saw that the assembly were taking his smear campaign
              seriously and were being taken in hook, line, and
              sinker, I figured that it was time to act.
  I said a quick prayer along the lines of, "By all the hoodwinking
              powers of chicanery, deceit, and fraud that be,
              especially those cunning ones who shaped my
              childhood, this little rat is not going to get away
              with that. Bless my tongue with blarney and
              ballyhoo."
  I had hardly finished mumbling the prayer when some character
              left a humongous fart to my right. Right, I say to
              myself, says I, the wind's on my side, so I
              squeezed my way through and let go: "Members
              of the ass-embly let me be the first to tell you the
              tremendous news about how the war has slashed
              the price of small fry."

You should have seen their faces. They could have kissed me,
        each and every one of them.
Then, to really land them, I leaked that they should buy every
        frying pan in the town, so no one else can fry up.
        They leaped up in a wave of applause. They were
        speechless. They opened and closed their mouths
        like dumb fish. I caught them, all right.
I knew Paphlagon was no fool either. He knew my game, and he
        knew what the assembly wanted also. He piped
        up: "Gentlemen, in the light of this fishy news
        let's offer a hundred oxen to the goddess in
        appreciation." The assembly took his bait.
As soon as I realized what this piranha was up to, I outbid him
        and hollered: "Let's offer two hundred." I
        mentioned that, maybe, they should offer a
        thousand goats as well to Artemis, but only if
        sardines are still the same price. I hooked the
        assembly again and drew them in.
Your man lost it as soon as he heard this. He made a lurch for
        me. The guards barely managed to drag him off.
        All the assembly were on their feet, nattering
        about the sardine situation.
He begged them to hold off and hear what the delegation from
        Sparta had to say about a peace treaty. But, in
        unison, they all hollered: "A peace treaty! Are
        you joking? They only want peace now that our
        sardines are so cheap. They can do a running
        jump. Let the war continue."   380
They called a halt to the meeting and scattered. I dashed out of
        there and rushed down to market to buy up all
        the leeks and onions in sight. I divvied them
        out to everyone I saw in the assembly, gratis, as
        seasoning for their sardines. They were over the
        moon and thought the sun shone out of my ass.
I won the ass-embly over completely and finally with a few
        leeks.

CHORUS
> Right on.
> You were born under a lucky star.
> You are bound to go far.
> The other chancer ain't got a chance.
> In every instance you beat the pants
> off him in chicanery and bullshit.
> But don't rest on your laurels. Look out.
> We're right behind you, old chap.   390
> Now run him off the face of the map.
> *(The circle opens and retreats behind the sausage seller as Paphlagon*
> *enters.)*

SAUSAGE SELLER
> Look, here comes Paphlagon, working himself into a tidal
> > wave to drown me in. Isn't he going to land on
> > his ass?

PAPHLAGON
> I'll land you if it kills me. You're past tense, buddy.

SAUSAGE SELLER
> O buddy, look, I'm shaking with terror.
> *(He dances about with his whole body shaking.)*
> You make me laugh. You are all wind.

PAPHLAGON
> If I can't swallow you whole and spit you out, then I'll throw my
> > hat at it.

SAUSAGE SELLER
> You're all threats. I'll swallow you whole, hat and all, and then
> > belch you up.

PAPHLAGON
> Well, eat my hat. I'll beat the hide off you and have the best seat
> > at your funeral.

SAUSAGE SELLER
>Ha, that's a laugh. The only seat you'll ever be entitled to now is a
>>back seat.
>*(He turns his behind to him and points to it.)*

PAPHLAGON
>That's it. I'll take no more. Your number is up. I'll have your guts
>>for dessert.   400

SAUSAGE SELLER
>Heavens, isn't he the joker. Your blood sugar level must be low.
>>You need a bite to eat. What about a bit of bread?

PAPHLAGON
>I'll rip you asunder with my bare hands.

SAUSAGE SELLER
>And I'll tear out the bread you stole from the city.

PAPHLAGON
>What gall! I'll drag you before Demos and you'll pay for all this.

SAUSAGE SELLER
>So you think that you have Demos in your pocket!

PAPHLAGON
>You got it. I know the kind of bread he likes.

SAUSAGE SELLER
>You throw him the crusts like a mean nurse. You chew his food
>>for him and place a morsel in his mouth, while
>>you swallow three quarters of it yourself.

PAPHLAGON
>And that's not all. Demos is like dough in my hands. I'll shape
>>him any way I desire.

SAUSAGE SELLER
>   Aren't you the big guy? I could do the same with my asshole.

PAPHLAGON
>   If you think you'll be known as the guy who shat on me in the
>   ass-embly, think again. Let's go to Demos for a
>   rematch.   410

SAUSAGE SELLER
>   You got it. No problem. I'm calling your bluff.
>   *(They knock at Demos' door.)*

PAPHLAGON
>   Demos, please come on.

SAUSAGE SELLER
>   Yes, please, father, do grace us.

PAPHLAGON
>   Dear Demos, please come out and see what I have to put
>   up with.

DEMOS *(from within)*
>   What's all the hullabaloo out there? Give me a break.
>   *(Demos opens the door.)*
>   Look what you've done. You've knocked my wreath right off
>   the door.
>   *(He sees Paphlagon.)*
>   What's the matter with you?

PAPHLAGON
>   I'm being molested by this dick and these other jerks, and it's all
>   because I'm trying to protect you.

DEMOS
>   But why? What's the story?

PAPHLAGON
Because I'm loyal to you. I love you like no other.   420

DEMOS *(to the sausage seller)*
And who are you?

SAUSAGE SELLER
I'm his rival, his opposite. I love you, but not like this character.
I'm true to you, like any good decent person, and
everything I do is for the good of you. You're like
one of those self-destructive guys. You never
choose wholesome men, but prefer to be screwed
by lowlifes the like of him.

PAPHLAGON
Everything I do is to protect the people's asses.

SAUSAGE SELLER
Really? Tell us how. Go on.

PAPHLAGON
Really. I'll tell you. I cut in on the Pylos generals and brought
Spartan prisoners back in irons.

SAUSAGE SELLER
And I cut in on the cook and ran off with the grub.

PAPHLAGON *(to Demos)*
Look, Demos. Excuse me, but you're no asshole. You can tell
which one of us is on your side. Go on, choose
between us.

SAUSAGE SELLER
That's right. You know best, but don't make your choice here.

DEMOS

What do you mean? Not here! Why not here? This is my place.
The assembly always meets here. Have you gone
mad? It's here or nowhere.

SAUSAGE SELLER *(to the audience)*

Oh blast, I've had it. This old codger is fine in his own home,
but here on these stony seats he can't tell his ass
from his elbow.   430

CHORUS *(to sausage seller)*

Now's your chance. All hands on deck.
Steer a straight course with gusto.
But just when you think you have Tricky Dick,
watch out, he's no dodo.
He can turn the tide his way in a jiffy.
This won't be plain sailing.
He'll try to outmaneuver your galley,
and you'll end up turtling.

SIMON

Get your grappling hook ready.

PAPHLAGON

Now I beg you, queen of the whole picture—   440
I who have been loyalest of Athenians,
next to Lysicles, the sheep-fucker,
and Cynna and Salabaccha, the courtesans
please allow me my usual place at the table
for doing . . . well . . . I suppose fuck-all,
but if I'm against you,
if I'm not true blue
unwilling to fight for you to the last breath,
then leather me—please, please—to death.

SAUSAGE SELLER

And if I don't adore and cherish you, then make mincemeat out
of yours truly.   450

PAPHLAGON

Demos, who, in the name of heaven, could love you more than
me? Who could have done more? From the very
word go I made you extraordinary profits by
squeezing every Tom, Dick, and Harry. If it
moved, I taxed it. I didn't give a damn about
them, and it's all for you.

SAUSAGE SELLER

Compared to me, Demos, such efforts are laughable. I'll steal
the last crust of bread from the homeless for you.
But what I want you to see is how this thief is just
feathering his own nest. You, who saved Attica at
Marathon, you, whose triumphs we love to extol,
look at yourself now. He has you sitting, piles
and all, on a cold, hard old stone.
Here, take this cushion that I've sewn especially for you. Lift your
big behind and slip this under your tush. Haven't
you put enough strain on your rear?

(He slips a cushion under Demos.)

DEMOS

My dear man, do tell me your name. You're not a descendant of
our greatest hit man, are you? At any rate, this
gesture indicates a patriot.

PAPHLAGON *(aside to sausage seller)*

You're some ass licker. You sure can pile it on.

SAUSAGE SELLER *(aside to Paphlagon)*

Well, you made an ass out of him with far less cheek.

PAPHLAGON

> Well, I'm prepared to put my ass on the line like no one before
> me. This I swear, when it comes to serving the
> people, I'm no bum.

SAUSAGE SELLER

> Such baloney. We all know how loyal you are to him and the
> people. For eight years you allowed droves of
> hicks to be driven into the city, his city. They had
> to hole up in old barrels and broken crates, in
> every nook and cranny of the town, and you
> haven't raised a finger. All you're interested in
> is keeping him diverted inside.

You've milked him and the city until the cows come home—
> and, of course, they never do. When the
> ambassadors of the enemy offered a peace treaty,
> you rubbed it in their faces and booted them up
> the runt.

PAPHLAGON

> Darn you—I was taking the longer view and thinking about
> what was best for him. I wasn't going to accept
> some itty-bitty treaty that, in the end, would only
> sink us deeper in the muck. No, this war must
> go on until he has all of Greece in his pocket.   460

The oracle says that if he sits tight he'll one day rule Arcadia and
> the whole evil empire and make a fortune out of
> it. Whatever happens, I'll take good care of him.

SAUSAGE SELLER

> You're some joker. You don't give a fiddler's damn about him
> ruling Arcadia. All you think about is how you
> can fiddle funds out of the military business.
> People are so taken up with the war they don't
> have a bull's notion of what you're up to. They're
> so blinkered that you have them eating out of
> your hands.

But if ever there is peace again, and Demos can go back to his
        place in the country, he'll cop how you've been
        fiddling him as soon as he gets his oats. Then,
        my lad, watch out. He'll be out for your hide.
But what am I saying? You know all this better than anyone, and
        that's why you pull the wool over his eyes and
        line your pockets on the sly.

PAPHLAGON

You have some cheek, talking to me like this and sullying my
        name in front of Demos and the whole city. I've
        done more for them than even Themistocles.

SAUSAGE SELLER

O citizens, would you listen to him? So now you're heads and
        shoulders above even Them-istocles. He found
        our city half flooded, so he built the harbor that
        we now fish in. While you, on the flip side, only
        want to wall us in with your pronouncements.
You have some nerve comparing yourself to Them-istocles,
        especially since he's in exile, while you're stuffing
        your face with fish pie.

PAPHLAGON

Demos, Demos, it's a crying shame that such things should be
        said by this character simply because I love you.
(He falls whimpering at Demos' feet.)

DEMOS

Shut up. You've thrown enough muck. All these years and I
        haven't seen what you've been up to. Get up off
        your filthy knees and quit groveling for truffles
        of pity, you swine.

SAUSAGE SELLER

Ah, dear sweet Demos, you've got his number at last. While your
        back was turned he devoured as much of the

public funds as he could get his hands on and
then washed it down with your own private
funds.   470

PAPHLAGON

You won't, you won't, you won't get away with this. I'll show how
you nibbled away at the city's bread.

SAUSAGE SELLER

Oh, come on, you're only rowing with one oar now. We all know
how you tried to drain the city dry, and I'll prove
how you took a bribe from Mytilene. My, my,
you'd do anything for money.

SIMON

What a talker. You're the cat's whiskers. If things keep going the
way they are, you'll be the greatest of all. You'll
rule the whole caboodle. You'll make a mint out
of it. But watch it. Don't get cocky. You have him
by the balls now. Blow him away.

PAPHLAGON

Now, gentlemen, don't count your chickens before they hatch.
I've still got something big up my sleeve that'll
shut the mouths of the anti-Paphlagon clan. I've
still got my Pylos shields. Ah!

SAUSAGE SELLER

Speaking of shields—hang on. Those shields give me a good grip
on you. If you love the people as much as you say
you do, then why did you hang up these shields
with their handles still on? Suspicious, ah? That's
sacrilege.
Demos, do you see what he's up to? If he smells any trouble from
you, then he'll call on his young groupies . . .
those apprentice leathermongers, along with the

cheese and honey merchants that are always
around. They've been scheming. As soon as he
thinks you're turning against him, he'll order
them to grab the shields off the wall.
Mark my words, this will all happen under cover of night. They'll
make a bolt for the granaries and take over.

DEMOS

Well, burst my britches, I didn't realize the shields had holds still
on them. That's illegal. You bastard, how long
have you been ripping me off and short-changing
the people?

PAPHLAGON

Gee, Demos, I beg you not to believe a word that comes out of
this guy's gob. Can't you see I'm the only man
who keeps taps on any troublemakers? I squash
anything that might be brewing.

SAUSAGE SELLER

Yup, you're like a guy fishing for eels. They have to rake up the
mud before they catch the fish. When everything
is calm they are out of luck. That's how you
work. You're always raking up the dirt to catch
us out.   480
And tell us this: of all the leather you sell, have you ever given
Demos a patch of leather to mend his soleless
shoes?

DEMOS

By heavens, that's right. He never has!

SAUSAGE SELLER

So, you are getting the message, Demos. You're no heel after all.
Here, have a look at the gift of a pair of shoes I've
got for you.

DEMOS

I must say, you've a great soul, a real patriot. You know what we
need from head to toe.

PAPHLAGON

Golly, isn't that soul-destroying, that a pair of old soles should
count for so much. How quickly everything I've
done for you slips your mind. Wasn't it I who
sent lecherous Gryttus on his heels?

SAUSAGE SELLER

Ah, isn't it a crying shame that you should go about sniffing out
poor boys, afraid they'll bugger you. And look
how often you have seen poor Demos without a
cloak, and you haven't lifted a finger to wrap
something over his shoulders, even at the height
of winter.
But I won't put up with seeing dear, little Demos so poorly clad.
Here, Demos, put that over your poor shoulders.
It'll keep you good and warm.

DEMOS

Not even Themistocles outdoes this guy, although he did come
up with the bright idea of the wall. Still, this guy
beats him hands down.

PAPHLAGON

You ape. Such monkey tricks.

SAUSAGE SELLER *(aside to Paphlagon)*

I'm just following your example. I'm like a guy who's so
desperate to take a leak he hasn't time to find his
own shoes among all the others at the door. He
slips on someone else's and rushes out to shake
the dew from the lily.   490

PAPHLAGON *(aside to sausage seller)*
Well, you won't outdo me in brown-nosing. I'm a great actor.
(to Demos)
> Here, Demos, hang this cloak over your shoulders and let this
> character go hang himself. He's just pissing in
> the wind.

DEMOS
> Ugh. Get that off me. What a stink of leather. It reeks to high
> heaven.

SAUSAGE SELLER
> Watch him. He's trying to stink you out, and it isn't the first time.
> Do you remember those beans that he imported
> into the city?

DEMOS
> Yes, of course.

SAUSAGE SELLER
> He made sure that they were sold stinking cheap, so that the
> whole assembly would scoff them and gas each
> other to death.

DEMOS
> Well, blow me, an old windbag gave me wind of this.

SAUSAGE SELLER
> And ain't it true that there was such a smell that you all turned
> yellow?

DEMOS
> Phew. He blew us away for sure.

PAPHLAGON
> You're a gas character all right. Government is like a big baby—
> an alimentary canal with a voracious appetite at

one end and no sense of responsibility at the
other. You're piling it on now.   500

SAUSAGE SELLER
And the goddess herself proclaimed that I'd drop you in it.

PAPHLAGON
If you think that you are going to get me off the throne, then you
have another thing coming. Relax, Demos. Sit
down on this throne, and I'll bring you so much
money you can wipe your bottom with it.

SAUSAGE SELLER
Disgusting. How uncouth. He's all wind. Don't mind him.
Instead, take this cream. It'll cure your piles.

PAPHLAGON
I'll make you young again. I'll pluck every gray hair from your
body down to your short and curlies.

SAUSAGE SELLER
Ah, you're still young. Don't take a tack of notice of this guy.
By the way, here's some witch hazel if the cream
doesn't work.

PAPHLAGON
Demos, wipe your snotty nose on my head, my bush.

SAUSAGE SELLER
What! He's as bald as a baby's ass. Here wipe your snot on my
fine mop of hair.

PAPHLAGON
Bald, my ass.
(to the sausage seller)
I'll sort you out. I'll assign you to some ship that'll eat up your
cash and sink you.

SAUSAGE SELLER

Such huffing and puffing. This guy is going to boil over. Turn down the gas.   510

PAPHLAGON

You'll pay through the nose for this. I'll register you among the filthy rich and squeeze the jewels off you.

SAUSAGE SELLER

I couldn't be bothered threatening you. I'll say this much, though, before you dash off to make some fishy deal with the Milesians and net a whale of a profit. As soon as you sit down to tuck into your usual big fry up, may the assembly call. In your anxiety to scoff the profits, may you choke on the bones.

SIMON

Heavens above. You can really dish it out. Right on.

DEMOS

You bet. This proves all the more that this guy is at the top of the pile, and what a pile it is. As for you, Paphlagon, I've had enough of your acting. You fed me a hill of beans, and I swallowed the lot. What were you trying to do, kill me? Now give me back the ring with my insignia that I gave you.

PAPHLAGON

Here, shove that up your you know where. I guarantee that whoever takes my place will really blow you away.

(He throws the ring back at Demos.)

DEMOS *(to himself)*

I'm positive this ring isn't mine. The seal is different. Hey, take a gander at this. I can't quite make it out.

(He hands it to the sausage seller.)

SAUSAGE SELLER
>Give me a look. What is your seal again?

DEMOS
>A fig stuffed with . . . my people . . . sorry . . . let me see . . .
>>yes, fat.

SAUSAGE SELLER
>Well, it isn't this one.

DEMOS
>So what is it?   520

SAUSAGE SELLER
>A foul gull screeching on top of a rock.

DEMOS
>What? No!

SAUSAGE SELLER
>Why?

DEMOS
>Get that out of my sight. He's been wearing the ring of
>>Cleonymus.
>*(He takes another ring from his pocket and gives it to the sausage seller.)*
>Here, put this on.

PAPHLAGON
>Stop. Please. Wait till you hear what I have to tell you about your
>>fortune.

SAUSAGE SELLER
>And I'll tell you a thing or two about it also.

PAPHLAGON
>If you let this guy palm you off, you're sure to go blind.

SAUSAGE SELLER
>And if you believe this play actor, he'll skin you alive, down to
>>the very stump.

PAPHLAGON
>My oracles say that you are going to be showered with roses and
>>rule the world.   530

SAUSAGE SELLER
>Mine says that you'll wear a purple robe and a crown, and that
>>you'll drive that wimp Smicythes and his ball and
>>chain out of the courts.

DEMOS *(to the sausage seller)*
>Go, get your oracles and let's hear them.

SAUSAGE SELLER
>It'll be my pleasure.

DEMOS *(to the audience)*
>Oh goody, goody.
>*(to Paphlagon)*
>Now don't think you're going to get a free ride. You fetch yours,
>>too, buddy.

PAPHLAGON
>Oh, all right, so.

SAUSAGE SELLER
>Right on. I'm all for this.
>*(He leaves with Paphlagon trailing reluctantly behind him.)*

SIMON
>If Paphlagon gets the boot, it'll be a great day for Athens, and
>>everyone else for that matter. I overheard some
>>codgers in the square say otherwise, but a pox on

them. They take Paphlagon's side. They insist
that if it wasn't for him, the city would be
without two of our most crackerjack tools: the
pestle and the wooden spoon.
But what kills me is his swinish education. Those who went to
school with him avow he could only tune his lyre
in the Dorian style. This crafty liar fooled us all
right.

PAPHLAGON *(returns weighed down with scrolls)*
Feast your eyes on all these. And there is more, believe it or not.   540

SAUSAGE SELLER *(returns carrying even more scrolls)*
Heavens, I could do with a good sit down, and there's a shit-
load more.

DEMOS
What are these?

PAPHLAGON
Your fortune.

DEMOS
You mean the whole lot?

PAPHLAGON
And there's tons more inside.

SAUSAGE SELLER
That's nothing. I've a whole building chockablock with them.

DEMOS
Where do they all come from?

PAPHLAGON
I got mine from the Boeotian fortune teller, Bakis.

DEMOS *(to the sausage seller)*
> And what about yours? Where did you get your star
> readings from?

SAUSAGE SELLER
> From the older brother of Bakis, from Fakis.   550

DEMOS *(to Paphlagon)*
> So, what's the story? What do they say? Start the star wars.

PAPHLAGON
> They're about the city, Pylos, you, me, the whole ball of wax.

DEMOS *(to the sausage seller)*
> And what does your lot say?

SAUSAGE SELLER
> Athens, lentil soup, the enemy, freshly caught fish, fishy traders,
> you, me . . . He'll be eating his words soon
> enough.

DEMOS
> Oh hurry up. Let's hear them, especially that one that says I'm
> going to be like a high-flying eagle.

PAPHLAGON
> Listen so, and take account of every word: "Son of Erechtheus,
> true Athenian, Apollo's words thunder from the
> Tripod in the sanctuary. He advises you to take
> care of the watchdog of the state. He can scare
> the pants off any trespasser. He is your main
> man. He'll hound the country for your money.
> Watch out because the daws that are out to croak
> him are really out to croak you."

DEMOS

>Huh! What was that all about? What's Erechtheus got to do with
>bloody dogs and daws?

PAPHLAGON

>Can't you see? I'm your faithful watchdog, frightening every
>thief off. The oracle is telling you to take care
>of this mutt.

SAUSAGE SELLER

>That's a load of doggerel. This doggoned whelp has got his teeth
>into those oracles and has gnawed away at them
>while your back was turned. He's only giving you
>the bare bones. I have the lot here, and I've dog-
>eared the pages he's chewed.

DEMOS

>Read them so, but first let me pick up a stone to ward off being
>bitten by his dogma.   560

SAUSAGE SELLER

>"Son of Erechtheus, watch out for that cur. He's taking you
>doggy-style for sure. He plays at being your lap
>dog, but as soon as you turn your head, he'll
>pounce on your grub and scoff the lot. And at
>night, while everyone is asleep, this do-gooder
>will simply trot into your kitchen and clean
>you out. He won't even leave you enough for
>a doggy bag."

DEMOS

>Well, I'll be a monkey's uncle. Fakis is top dog.

PAPHLAGON

>Please. I'm no dog's body. Give me a dog's chance and listen to
>this one. Please, master. You can decide what you
>want to do after hearing it: "There is a woman in

sacred Athens who will give birth to a lion. This
lion will curtail any cur who thinks that he can
take over and ride the city. He'll defend it like
he'd defend his very own cubs. Take care of him
and build a sturdy wooden wall with iron
towers."
Do you get it?

DEMOS

Doggone, I haven't a dog's chance of understanding what you're
barking about.

PAPHLAGON

Why, it's clear. The heavens are telling you to look after me,
your lion.

DEMOS

You're lying, all right. You've fooled me with all your lionizing.
I never noticed that I was in the lion's mouth all
the time.

SAUSAGE SELLER

There's a lion's share of this that he hasn't explained. You see that
bit where Apollo is telling you to build walls and
towers to keep this beast?

DEMOS

Yes, but what exactly does it mean?

SAUSAGE SELLER

Why, he was telling you to lock this animal up.   570

DEMOS

Well, that's one oracle that's about to come true.

PAPHLAGON

Don't take any of notice of all his crowing, or else you'll have to
eat crow.
(He starts reading another oracle quickly.)

"No—Take good care of your kite. He snatched the fishy
        Spartans and carried them back to you."

SAUSAGE SELLER
    Big deal. He's a high flyer, all right. He only pulled that off
            because he was high as a kite. O son of Cecrop,
                don't be so green and easily taken by this bird.
    If we were all really in trouble, then this old bird would be the
            first to fly the coop.

PAPHLAGON
    Oh, but listen to this. This oracle is the clincher:
(In his panic he rushes his words and "Pylos" sounds like "piles.")
    "There is a Pile-loss before Piles . . ."

DEMOS
    What? This is all a pain in the ass. A pile-loss before piles? I have
            piles. What's he piling on about? Ass licker.

SAUSAGE SELLER
    He saying that he's going to take care of your Pyl . . .

DEMOS
    He's not going to touch my piles. I'll manage my own bunch of
            grapes, thank you very much.   580

SAUSAGE SELLER
    That's right. That fox is all sour grapes. But pay attention to his
            oracle. It's about your fleet.

DEMOS
    Sure thing. Read it. What interests me most is how you're going
            to pay my navy.

SAUSAGE SELLER
>"Son of Aegeus, watch the dog-fox. He'll take you from behind
>and pretend he's just licking your ass. Then
>he'll make a swift run for it after he's cleaned
>you out."

Do you get it?

DEMOS
>Sure. That's Philotratus, that painted pimp, the Dogfox himself.
>He likes to do it doggy style and slip away as
>quickly as possible afterward.

SAUSAGE SELLER
>No. No. It's about that coffer-collecting fleet that this guy
>*(points at Paphlagon)*
>has been after you to cough up. Apollo won't allow it.

DEMOS
>How can you compare the fleet with a dog-fox?

SAUSAGE SELLER
>They're both fast. Right?

DEMOS
>So why is the fox called a dog-fox?   590

SAUSAGE SELLER
>Why? Of course because a dog and a ship are fleet.

DEMOS
>But where does the fox bit come in so?

SAUSAGE SELLER
>Well, because both the marines and the fox like to eat green
>grapes.

DEMOS

So where are the greenbacks for the young foxes?

SAUSAGE SELLER

I'll come up with it in less than three days. I swear.
(He takes out another oracle.)
But listen to this oracle. Apollo warns you to be leery of the city
of the palm.

DEMOS

The city of the palm?

SAUSAGE SELLER

The god is well able to read this guy's greasy palm.

PAPHLAGON

That's not true. Apollo is talking about that renowned
backhander Diopeithes. But I have another
oracle here that will send you over the moon.
You are to become an eagle and rule over all
the land.

SAUSAGE SELLER

That's nothing compared to this one. I have one that declares that
you'll rule over the land and sea, and that you'll
hold court in Ecbatana, where you'll have your
cake and be able to eat it too.   600

PAPHLAGON

Well, I dreamed that Athena herself would bless the country with
prosperity and well-being.

SAUSAGE SELLER

And I dreamed that our goddess emerged from the Acropolis
with an owl above her helmet. She poured
ambrosia over your head, Demos, and over
that dick she poured garlic pickle.

DEMOS
>Ah, there's no one smarter than Fakis.
>
>*(to the sausage seller)*
>>From now on you can take care of me in my old age and fill me
>>in on everything that's going on.

PAPHLAGON
>Wait a sec. Please. Give me a chance to take care of your daily
>needs and come up with horn, sorry, corn,
>especially for you.

DEMOS
>Enough. You've abused me long enough. You and The-o-pain-ass
>and all the rest of your flock have fleeced me.

PAPHLAGON
>But I'll get you your oats.

SAUSAGE SELLER
>He's pissing into a gale. I'll get you your oats and come up with
>a dish for you on the side as well. All you have
>to do is enjoy it.

DEMOS
>All right, put your money where your mouth is. I'll hand over the
>keys of the city to whichever one of you comes
>out on top.

PAPHLAGON
>I'm going to get there first.   610

SAUSAGE SELLER
>That's what you think.
>*(He pushes Paphlagon out of the way and rushes into the house
>before him.)*

CHORUS

Demos, you're a real humdinger. Look how men are at your beck
and call, so why do you give them such a free
ride? You love to be scratched and cajoled. You
belong to anyone who rubs you up the right way.
The lights are on, but there's no one at home.

DEMOS

That's what you think. I'm at home all right. I'm only letting on
that I'm an easy ride. I get such pleasure each day
taking all this in. I purposely set up a scoundrel
to be my prime minister. Then, when the time is
ripe and he's as big as he can get, I'll screw him.

CHORUS

Why, we're flabbergasted. You've taken the lot of us in. It's we've
been the asses. You couldn't have pulled it off any
better. You have been fattening up these dicks all
along like sacrifices on the Pnyx. When you're
short of a bit of meat you have one or the other
for starters.

DEMOS

You bet your bottom drawer I do. Just watch me. I'll catch them
yet. I'm no sucker. They think that they're streets
ahead of me, but I'm only giving them rope to
hang themselves with. I've been letting on that
I'm like a blind man holding out my hat, but I've
been keeping a sharp eye on those brats.
The next time they steal whatever's in the hat, I'll stuff it down
their throats and they'll throw up everything
they've robbed.
*(Paphlagon and the sausage seller return from different sides and collide
with each other.)*

PAPHLAGON
Get out of my way, or you're dead meat.

SAUSAGE SELLER
Get out of my way, you dead-beat.

PAPHLAGON
Demos, look how I've been waiting here for ages to serve you.

SAUSAGE SELLER
Don't take any notice of that moron. He has no patience and he's
always blowing things out of proportion. If he's
been waiting for ages, then I've been waiting for
ages and ages and . . .   620

DEMOS
And I've been waiting here ten times longer. You both really
cheese me off.

SAUSAGE SELLER
Ah, doesn't cheese improve with aging? Do you want me to tell
you what you should do now?

DEMOS
Yes, of course. Come on, come on. Spit it out. Don't keep us all
on tenterhooks.

SAUSAGE SELLER
Chalk a starting line and let the two of us begin from there, and
then we'll see who's top dog.

DEMOS
Chalk it down.
(One of the chorus draws a line.)
Get on your marks.
(Sausage seller and Paphlagon go to the starting line.)

PAPHLAGON AND SAUSAGE SELLER
Okay, ready.
(They take their marks.)

DEMOS
Take your mark, get set, go.
(The two race into the house.)

SAUSAGE SELLER
Hey, no cutting across me!
(They disappear inside.)

DEMOS
Well, by heaven, if I don't get my way today, I'll really have to
play hard to get.   630

PAPHLAGON *(as he returns)*
Take note of this. I was the first to bring you a chair.

SAUSAGE SELLER *(entering)*
A chair, my ass. What he needs is a table. Here you go, Demos.
(The two start rummaging frantically in their bags for food for Demos.)

PAPHLAGON
Look, here are plenty of hot oats. The Pyles remedy. They'll keep
you so regular nothing will be able to stop you.

SAUSAGE SELLER
And I've come up with specially baked bread, shaped the way our
own goddess likes it herself.
(He pulls out a long phallic baguette of bread from his trousers).

DEMOS
First Lady, I never realized she liked it so big. Wow. Give us a feel
of it.

PAPHLAGON
> Look, here is my scrumptious, creamy pea soup that was stirred
> > by the great hand of the First Lady herself.

SAUSAGE SELLER
> Demos, this is definite proof that she's taking care of you. Look
> > how she holds a pot of gravy over you.

DEMOS
> Sure she does, and you want to join the gravy train. Do you think
> > that the city would survive if she didn't hold her
> > pot over us?

PAPHLAGON
> And here's some fish as well. It was caught by the goddess who
> > scares the pants off her enemies.

SAUSAGE SELLER
> And from the number one daughter of the Almighty himself,
> > here is a succulent steak along with some blood
> > pudding and tripe.   640

DEMOS *(puffed up)*
> She's just thanking me for the shawl I sent her to keep her warm.

PAPHLAGON
> The goddess with the great boobs bids you to eat this pudding.
> > You'll row all the better for it.
(aside)
> With one oar!

SAUSAGE SELLER
> Now get a load of this as well. This will put hairs on your chest
> > and warm the cockles of your heart.
(aside)
> And keep you busy trying to fart.

DEMOS
And what am I supposed to do with this tripe?

SAUSAGE SELLER
Our goddess has dispatched it to you to feed your navy. You
know how she's so disposed toward your fleet.
Here take a slug of this. Two-fifths of it is wine,
and the rest water.

DEMOS *(drinks)*
Heavens above, this mix sure hits the spot.

SAUSAGE SELLER
Yes, it was concocted by no less than the heady daughter of the
Almighty Father.

PAPHLAGON
Here, try this slice of cake.   650

SAUSAGE SELLER
A piece of cake, how are you! Here's a whole cake.

PAPHLAGON *(aside to the sausage seller)*
Ah, but I've some hare stew for him. You'll never be able to find
that here.

SAUSAGE SELLER *(to the audience)*
I'm in a right stew now! Where am I going to find hare? I'll have
to pull off some harem-scarem trick.

PAPHLAGON
Here. You're cooked now. Take a long look at this hare.

SAUSAGE SELLER
I don't care. Here. Here. Look who's on their way here.
(He points in a direction behind Paphlagon's back.)

PAPHLAGON
    Who?

SAUSAGE SELLER
    Why, it's an envoy loaded with dough.

PAPHLAGON
    Bread! Spondulics! Moolah! Where? Where?
(He turns quickly to see.)

SAUSAGE SELLER
    Here. Here. Let them through here.
(He grabs the hare stew as soon as Paphlagon turns his back to look around.)
    Now, Demos, me old buddy, look at this hare stew I got for you. 660

PAPHLAGON *(quickly turns back, realizing how he's been duped)*
    You hustler. You've ripped me off.

SAUSAGE SELLER
    Yup. I've just taken a leaf from you. You ripped off the men at
        Pylos.

DEMOS *(to the sausage seller)*
    How did you come up with that bluff so quickly? You're on the
        ball. It was a doozy. You're a real genius, all right.

SAUSAGE SELLER
    I got the idea from our First Lady. All I had to do was pull it off.

PAPHLAGON
    Darn, and after I broke my ass getting it.

SAUSAGE SELLER
    But it was I who cooked up how to present it to Demos.

DEMOS *(to Paphlagon)*
>   Get outta here. The only guy that interests me is the guy who
>   hands it to me on a plate.

PAPHLAGON
>   God almighty. He's boiled me alive all right.

SAUSAGE SELLER
>   Why, Demos, can't you distinguish which of us is better for you
>   and your belly?

DEMOS
>   I can, but I need to come up with some way of making it
>   convincing for everyone. Have you any bright
>   ideas?   670

SAUSAGE SELLER
>   I have. All you need to do is have a quick look in my bag and in
>   Paphlagon's. Then compare what is in each of
>   them. You'll have all the proof in the world there.

DEMOS *(looks in sausage seller's bag)*
>   Let me have a gander in here. What have you got?

SAUSAGE SELLER
>   O father, can't you see it's completely empty? I've given you lock,
>   stock, and barrel.

DEMOS
>   Why, you're a real man of the people, all right.

SAUSAGE SELLER
>   Now take a glance in Paphlagon's bag of tricks. A quick peek is all
>   you need.

DEMOS *(looks in Paphlagon's bag)*
> Well, what do you know! It's still full of goodies. Look at that
> > huge cake, and he was only going to give me a
> > lousy slice of it.

SAUSAGE SELLER
> That's him all over. He's kept the larger portion for himself on
> > the sly.

DEMOS *(to Paphlagon)*
> You rotter. Is this the way you treat me after I've crowned you
> > and poured gifts on you?

PAPHLAGON
> No. No. It was for the good of the city that I stole.

DEMOS
> Give me back that crown I gave you in Sphacteria. I'll crown this
> > man with it now.   680

SAUSAGE SELLER
> Drop it, you ingrate.

PAPHLAGON
> No, wait. I have an oracle here that tells exactly who is going to
> > give me the boot.

SAUSAGE SELLER
> All right. Spout it out. It can't be anyone else but my good self.

PAPHLAGON
> Okay, so, but first let's test you to see if the oracle agrees with
> > you. My first question is, where did you go to
> > school when you were a lad?

SAUSAGE SELLER
  I was beaten and battered like dough in the baker's kitchen.

PAPHLAGON
  What?
(aside)
  Gee, this is exactly what my oracle says.
(to the sausage seller)
  And what training did they give you to beat you into shape and
        make you hard?

SAUSAGE SELLER
  They taught me how to pilfer left, right, and center, and go about
        as if butter wouldn't melt in my mouth.

PAPHLAGON *(aside)*
  Apollo, what in heaven's name are you trying to do to me?   690
(to the sausage seller)
  After that apprenticeship what did you do?

SAUSAGE SELLER
  I stole sausages and, well, sometimes I even took a bit of meat up
        the back.

PAPHLAGON *(aside)*
  Oh, no. I'm done for now, fucked completely. Maybe I still have
        one small chance.
(to the sausage seller)
  Tell us this much. Did you do your business in the city center or
        at the entrance?

SAUSAGE SELLER
  Why, didn't I tell you I sold my salted meat at the back entrance?

PAPHLAGON

O heavens. The oracle is true. I'm baked. Carry out the stretcher before I go bottom up.

(He reluctantly takes off his crown.)

Best of luck, my darling. Our time is up. All the best. I'll pass it on to some other swine, but I swear there's no greater swindler than me. He's just got luck on his side. That lucky duck! Oh fuck, I'm a dead duck.

(He throws himself down weeping.)

SAUSAGE SELLER *(takes the crown)*

Zeus, only for you I'd never have pulled it off.

(Demosthenes, who has been watching off stage all along, rushes back when he sees that the sausage seller is sure to win. He addresses the sausage seller fawningly.)

DEMOSTHENES

Well done. You did it. But remember that you'd never have pulled this off if it weren't for me. The one thing that I ask, and it isn't much, is that you make me your secretary like Phanus.

(Demosthenes is tolerated but ignored.)

DEMOS *(to the sausage seller)*

And now tell us your real name?   700

SAUSAGE SELLER

Agoracritus, a square liar . . . I mean lawyer.

DEMOS

Well then, Agoracritus, you're the right man for the job. I'll leave everything to you. And while you're at it, take care of Paphlagon.

AGORACRITUS

> Sit back now, Demos. Relax. I'll make sure you're nice and
> > comfy. Everyone will see how I'm the best man
> > for the job. I'll take care of feeding the city's big
> > mouths.

(Agoracritus leads Demos off with his arm over his shoulder.)

CHORUS

> What better way to start
> or finish this song
> than to sing of great riders
> who gallop their steeds
> around the arena.
> We won't mention Lysistratus,
> nor poor homeless Thumantis,   710
> who, dear God, can be seen
> holding his cup out at Delphi,
> crying his eyes out.
> He clings to your quiver, begging
> you to put him out of his misery.

SIMON

> Don't misunderstand us, there's nothing wrong now with
> > attacking the wasters and chancers who aim to
> > bring down the city. If anything it shows how
> > worthy the new guy is and shows what he's up
> > against.
> Everyone knows good Arignotus, but what about his brother
> > Ariphrades? They're like chalk and cheese. He's
> > about as rotten as they come. Rotten isn't good
> > enough to describe this pervert. He's riding the
> > whole town.
> He's even come up with a few kinky tricks of his own that I'm . . .
> > em . . . too em-barr-assed to describe. Something
> > about taking golden showers all over his
> > lecherous face and something called brown
> > nosing or brown showers, something vile. He's

supposed even to force gerbils up his you know
where . . . while all the while this Gerbelonymus
plays with his flute. Oh, it's enough to make
you puke.

I tell you he's so vile, I wouldn't even take a drink with any of
his mates. If he's around I'd keep my back to
the wall.

CHORUS

How often have you lain awake at night,   720
tossing and turning,
trying to figure out where in the world
Cleonymus puts it all?
He eats even the wealthy men
so out of house and home
that they end up begging him
to leave, at least, the table.
Maybe he's got a tapeworm.

PANAETIUS

You know that we've heard that the council met recently and one
of the elder women stood up and asked, "Are any
of you aware that a certain mate of Paphlagon,
Hyperbolus, is asking to take a hundred women
to Carthage? That depraved big-mouth. Can you
believe it?"

The whole assembly denounced him. One young slip of a thing,
who hasn't been sailed by a man yet, declared,
"He won't row my boat that's for sure. I'll rot
first."   730

Another cried, "He's out to rape us and tie us in bondage. I'll
sail to the sanctuary of the Furies before I let him
shiver me timbers. If he thinks he can treat the
city like this, he has something else coming. Let
him sink his own bloody ship."

(Agoracritus returns, dressed in regalia.)

AGORACRITUS

>Let everyone relax and not utter another foul word. Call no more witnesses, shut down the courts, the very pride of the city. And, in honor of our good fortune, let us raise the roof with song.

PANAETIUS

>Bearer of the torch of sacred Athens, savior of our islands, tell us why exactly the streets should be blessed with meat?

AGORACRITUS

>I poured a rich dressing on Demos and made him more presentable.

SIMON

>You're amazing all right, but where is he?

AGORACRITUS

>Why, of course, he's here in Athens, our fair Athens, that is crowned now with flowers.

CHORUS

>How will we know him? What does he look like if he's changed so much? What sort of character is he now?

AGORACRITUS

>Let me share this good news with you. He's the same as he was in the good old days, when Aristeides and Miltiades lived with him. Look for yourself. I hear him coming.

(sings)

>"Happy days are here again."

>Welcome the return of Athens of old. The renowned home of Demos is worthy of poem and song once more.   740

CHORUS
     O fair Athens, beautiful city
     charming and pretty,
     crowned with flowers, enviable city,
     show us the king of this country.
(Demos is brought in on a portable throne. He is dressed in magnificent
                              regalia and looks younger.)

AGORACRITUS
     Would you take a look at the man himself.
     He's wearing a cricket hair band.
     He's dressed to kill and smells grand.
     He is the essence of peace itself.

CHORUS
     Welcome, king of the Greeks.
     We bow to you and are happy for you.   750
     Your joy is worthy of Athens, the prize of Marathon.
(Demos descends from his throne.)

DEMOS
     Agoracritus, my good man, come here. You decked me out well.

AGORACRITUS
     I sure did. If you could only see what you looked like up to this
                    and what kind of an impression you made, then
                    you'd think me a god.

DEMOS
     Tell me, what was I really like?

AGORACRITUS
     Well, first and foremost, when any dog's body showed up at the
                    assembly and said, "Demos, my dear, I truly love
                    you and am the only one who really cares for you
                    and your safety," then you stuck out your breast

like a cock and brandished your horns like a big,
   bloody bull.

DEMOS
   Really?

AGORACRITUS
   And then this guy would leave the assembly with you in his
      pocket.

DEMOS
   You're not serious? Was I that blind?

AGORACRITUS
   You were. You should have seen yourself. Your ears would
      open and close like an umbrella on a
      showery day.

DEMOS
   Was I that senile?   760

AGORACRITUS
   Yes, honestly. When two speakers made proposals at the
      assembly, one to build good ships, the other to
      spend oodles of money on state bureaucracy, the
      bureaucrats would win hands down every time.
      Now, why do you look so downcast?

DEMOS
   I'm mortified. I've made a right mess of everything.

AGORACRITUS
   Oh, stop now, you weren't really to blame. It was these characters
      who hoodwinked you. They're the culprits. Now,
      if some gangster comes along and said, "There
      are no provisions for you unless you convict the
      fellow," what would you say to him now?

DEMOS

I'd have him flung out of the court. I'd wrap Hyperbolus around
his neck and fling him from the cliff at the back
of the Acropolis.

AGORACRITUS

Now you're talking. That's the right policy, but how do you
propose dealing with everything else?

DEMOS

First and foremost, as soon as the navy docks, I'll pay every sailor
in full.

AGORACRITUS

That'll soften any hard ass.

DEMOS

After that, I won't allow the name of any infantryman to be
transferred to some cushy number on the quiet.
He'll have to stay put.

AGORACRITUS

That'll catch Cleonymus, all right.

DEMOS

And I'll ban anyone from the agora who hasn't a beard.   770

AGORACRITUS

Then what'll become of those boys: smooth-cheeked Cleisthenes
and Strato?

DEMOS

I'm really only thinking about those asses hanging around the
perfume shops, mouthing off stuff like "Phaeax
is such a smart ass. How cunningly he wangled
his way out of the death penalty. How brilliant

and incisive; how original and persuasive. He
was able to outmaneuver any objection."

AGORACRITUS
So you are not going to kowtow to those two pups?

DEMOS
No, indeed. I'll hound them into doing something practical for a
change.

AGORACRITUS *(beckoning a lad to come from inside with a stool)*
If that's the case, then take this chair. It's yours along with this
big boy
(aside to Demos)
with the big lad to cart it around for you. You can take it anytime
you want.

DEMOS *(sings)*
Hallelujah.
Happy days are here again—
The sky is blue
(aside as he points at the lad)
and I'll screw you—   780
Happy days are here again.

AGORACRITUS
You can be sure of that as soon as I hand over the thirty-year
peace treaty.
(He calls into the house. Two young women rush out.)
These are the peace terms. Come. On your knees.
*(They kneel at the feet of Agoracritus and Demos and look from the
audience as if they are performing fellatio on
Agoracritus and Demos. Aside to Demos.)*
You've heard of course why I wear drawers?

DEMOS
No, why?

AGORACRITUS
To keep my ankles warm.
(Agoracritus and Demos guffaw.)

DEMOS
Well blow me, they're delightful. Please tell me they're mine, all
mine. Can I do anything I want with them?
Where did you find them?

AGORACRITUS
Wouldn't you know. Paphlagon had them locked up in his own
place. He foamed at the mouth at the very sight
of them. He kept them in bondage, all for
himself. I had to have them, but I'm giving them
to you now. You can have them anywhere you
want in the country.

DEMOS
And what do you plan for Paphlagon, who is so guilty?

AGORACRITUS
Oh, I won't be too hard. I'll make him take over my old job. He'll
have to trade sausages at the city entrance. I'll
make him pimp his sausage and hold commerce
with the queens of the night and drink nothing
but piss-water.   790

DEMOS
You've definitely come up with the right punishment. He's only
fit for the gutter. And, in return for all your
blessings, I'll invite you to take your place at the
Prytaeum. Here, shove on this toady cloak and

follow me. Let someone else take him. He'll be
exposed in front of every stranger he rode. We'll
make a holy show of him.

*(Demos, Agoracritus, the lad with the chair, and the Female Peace Terms
go out one side, followed by Demosthenes, Simon,
Panaetius, and the rest of the chorus singing a
version of "Happy Days Are Here Again."
Paphlagon, now dressed in the sausage seller's old
working clothes, is carried out the other side on the
sausage seller's old wagon. He starts to wake just as
they exit and leaves a terrible moan-cum-cry.)*

Clouds

Translated by
Carol Poster

Translator's Preface

The task of a translator is one of making choices—about interpretation of the original text and about the nature of the English work being produced. By necessity, these choices are highly individual ones. No two translators of Aristophanes are likely to produce identical versions. In fact, the numerous previous translations of *Clouds* differ so much that many lines look as though they might have been derived from entirely different originals. The purpose of this Preface, therefore, is to explain what choices I have made as a translator specifically as choices rather than as absolute characteristics of the play, as a sort of *caveat lector*.

Cicero discusses some of the choices facing translators in terms of a distinction between what he terms grammatical and oratorical translation. For him, grammatical translation is the literal word-for-word rendition students are trained to perform in elementary language classes. Oratorical translation, what we now might term literary translation, focuses on carrying over the spirit but not necessarily the letter of the original work. Each translation thus represents a set of choices, some along the grammatical-oratorical spectrum, and some grounded in more complex interpretive issues.

The translator of Aristophanes also needs to make certain decisions unlikely to confront translators of modern drama. The Greek texts of Aristophanes derive from a complex manuscript tradition, involving numerous medieval manuscripts, papyri, early printed editions, commentaries (*scholia*), and quotations in other authors. Although the variations among manuscripts are not drastic in the sense of differing with respect to gross plot elements, there are numerous minor verbal differences, from which translators must choose, and one other major set of difficulties. The original manuscripts did not include any stage directions, nor did they clearly indicate which lines were assigned to which speakers. For stage directions, I have supplied them in order to clarify what I think might be happening in the play; readers should be aware that these are my own conjectures, and not present in the Greek text. For distribution of lines among characters, most cases are quite obvious; for the remaining ones, as well as for the overall text, I have generally followed K. J. Dover's edition, with the exception of accepting a few of W. J. M. Starkie's conjectures, which, though a bit weaker on textual grounds, seemed to me as fitting better with the logic of the speeches, and thus more readily translatable.

Even beyond the textual problems, translating Aristophanes is a difficult task and creating, in accordance with the aims of the Penn Greek Drama series, an actable translation of *Clouds* verges on the impossible. The first difficulty a translator encounters is caused by the nature of Aristophanic humor. Many of the jokes are highly topical puns, relying for effect on detailed knowledge of Athenian politics and slang. A good way to illustrate the problems caused by the specificity of this sort of humor is by examining a joke which could be considered a modern analogue to those of Aristophanes:

"What is the difference between the *Titanic* and President Clinton?"
"We know how many people went down on the *Titanic*."

This joke, which appeared in several variants on the Internet in spring 1998, is not, to a contemporary American reader, particularly abstruse or arcane. It depends on common knowledge and an obvious pun. Imagine, however, just how many difficulties would be encountered by a professor of twentieth-century American studies telling it to students in A.D. 4400. The professor would need to explain:

· Clinton was an American President who, during the period the joke was in circulation, was being investigated for various sexual misadventures.
· The popular American news media during this period purveyed extensive coverage of all facets of the investigation into Clinton's sexual habits.
· In American culture during this period, a substantial portion of the population believed that (1) married men should not have sexual relationships with people other than their wives and (2) politicians' sexual mores and activities were important factors in their qualifications for their offices.
· The *Titanic* was an ocean liner that sank in 1912.
· During the period in which the joke was being told, several popular books and films had been released about the sinking of the *Titanic*.

· In American English of this period, "go down on" was used as a slightly vulgar euphemism for "perform oral sex."

If the original version of the joke is only mildly funny, the reconstructed and footnoted version is utterly humorless.

The general question that faces all translators of Aristophanes is how one can preserve the humor despite cultural distance. One approach is transposition, using topical contemporary jokes in place of ancient Athenian ones. There are, for me, two fatal problems with such a move. The first is that Aristophanes was not a twentieth-century American, and recent topical jokes invoke cultural paradigms incompatible with the assumptions underlying the plays. If one took as an example the joke about Clinton and the *Titanic*, it is highly unlikely that any Athenian would have considered impeaching an elected official on the grounds that said official had occasionally engaged in sexual activities with one or more people (female or male) other than his wife, unless such acts jeopardized a diplomatic mission or had some other quite direct bearing upon the political situation. A casual liaison with a flute girl, for example, would only have been worthy of comic mention for the obvious innuendo. The second problem with transposition of jokes into a recent context is that topical humor has a very short shelf life; jokes popular as I write this Preface in 1998 will appear dated by the time this volume appears in 1999, and might well be incomprehensibly old-fashioned to a reader in 2005 or 2020.

Another possible approach to translation of Aristophanes is a scholarly one, ignoring the aesthetic dimensions of the play and attempting a literal translation, liberally studded with notes and commentary. Starkie's prose translation, for example, does a quite commendable job of giving a side-by-side version relatively accurately (except for the lewder jokes) with extensive notes. For the reader who knows some Greek and is looking for help with the more difficult passages, such an approach is quite valuable, but for the Greekless reader it misses the point. Aristophanes is funny and his plays are written in carefully crafted verse. Slightly stilted academic prose gives a very inaccurate impression of his work.

Since the avowed purpose of this collection is to produce actable twentieth-century versions of the plays, I have chosen to do a verse translation that remains relatively close to the Greek in general outline, without attempting the hyperliteral word-for-word accuracy which, though perhaps appropriate to Aristotle, would result in something unreadable as well as unactable. I have used a few different approaches to the problem of topicality. The first is what Burton Raffel has termed the "embedded footnote"; that is, I have occasionally added a few explanatory words or even lines to clarify jokes that might prove incomprehensible to any but professional Hellenists. Occasionally I preserve the specific circumstances of the Greek but sacrifice the humor; at other points, I preserve the humor by blurring the specificity of detail. While I would prefer to have some very elaborate justification for where I used which strategy, in most cases the best explanation I can supply is that it sounded good to me at the time.

There is only one set of jokes for which I deliberately took substantial liberties with the text. At lines 733–54 (660–70 in the Greek), Aristophanes makes a series of jokes based on a possible confusion between the natural and grammatical genders of "chicken" and "trough." Since English lacks grammatical gender, the humor simply does not translate. To further complicate the issue, "chickens" are among the few birds in English that can be distinguished by gender using quite common terms, "rooster" and "hen." In order to clarify the verbal issue concerning gender, I have transformed the chickens into "ducks," which do not have common gender-specific terms in English. I retain the ducks for the echoing of the same joke at 920–26 (Greek 847–54), and bring them in again for the set of jokes at 1349–52 (Greek 1248–59). These jokes, which in the Greek concern troughs and actually repeat jokes from 660–70, depend for their humor simultaneously on grammatical gender, classical Greek methods of making bread, and an obscene pun (also used in Aristophanes' *Peace*) concerning mortars and pestles—a combination I found impossible to reproduce in anything resembling comprehensible English. I suspect that in production the potential visual humor of having live ducks on stage could compensate for omission of this very language-specific piece of verbal humor.

In addition to difficulties common to Aristophanic humor in general, *Clouds* confronts both reader and translator with a quite complex set of problems unique to its specific nature and circumstances of production. *Clouds* was originally presented at the City Dionysia in 423 B.C., where it won third (i.e., last) prize. Aristophanes, disappointed by the lukewarm reception of what he appears to have considered the best of his plays, revised *Clouds*, and the text we have is not the original but the revised version. The nature and extent of the revisions, and whether the revised version was actually performed or even intended for performance, have been the subject of considerable scholarly debate.

Both questions concerning the revisions of *Clouds* and those concerning the somewhat puzzling structure of the play revolve around a section known as the *parabasis* (lines 568–695), where the Chorus addresses the audience directly, even speaking (lines 568–617) in the assumed persona of the playwright himself. What makes the parabasis so puzzling is that it appears to be making claims that are undermined by the rest of the play. Aristophanes claims that *Clouds* is the most chaste of his plays, that it avoids the crude portrayals of *phalloi* and the obscene *cordax* dances of his rivals' plays, and eschews jokes about bald heads, old men beating people with canes, and large fires. Many of the things the parabasis claims have been avoided in *Clouds* in fact occur. One hypothesis that has been advanced to account for this apparent contradiction is that the revision of *Clouds* was only partially completed, a solution that involves assuming that a partial and clumsy private revision would have substantially wider circulation than a version performed at a highly visible festival and possibly available in standardized written form. Instead, I think the parabasis, rather than contradicting the rest of the play, provides us with a key for understanding it.

The parabasis claims that *Clouds* was the most chaste of Aristophanes' plays. This claim may be true of the earlier *Clouds*. Since, however, the text is not extant, we cannot judge the veracity of the assertion. The claim of chastity is also true of the portion of the revised *Clouds* prior to the parabasis (lines 1–567); with the exception of a few relatively mild flatulence jokes, the humor is relatively sober, restrained, and intellectual. Immediately after Aristophanes makes his claims of sober and chaste humor, however, he begins to undercut them. At line 601 he says he won't cheat audiences with the same play given again and again, even though the current version of *Clouds*, being the *second* or revised version, does precisely that. He says that he'll now refrain from attacking Cleon (line 604), but he begins attacking Cleon at lines 646–55, and his numerous jokes about Cleonymus might well play with the similarity of the names. His refusal to attack Hyperbolus (606–15), in actuality is an attack on Hyperbolus employing the rhetorical figure of *praeteritio*, and is followed by direct attack at lines 690–92. Next, at lines 779–816, there is an extended series of masturbation jokes, relying heavily on the visual humor of precisely the red-tipped leather *phalloi*

Aristophanes said were excluded from the play. An old man not only beats others with a whip (1400–1404), but also is beaten by his own son (1420–27). *Clouds* then ends with a huge fire and the very weeping and wailing that was condemned in the parabasis. Rather than try to explain the relationship between the humor of the play and the claims of the parabasis in terms of various unprovable theories concerning reproduction of the text of *Clouds* in some unspecified state of partial revision, I think it might be possible to assume that the violations of the strictures of the parabasis are deliberate, and done for comic effect; that is, Aristophanes is both showing us that he is, in fact, capable of writing precisely the sort of "coarse, crude, vulgar, simpleminded piece of slapstick" (line 576) promulgated by his rivals, and doing so much better at it than his rivals that he can, as he perpetuates their tradition, simultaneously satirize it.

The parabasis marks a turning point not only in the character of the comedy with which we are presented, but also in the nature and behavior of the play's central comic character, Strepsiades. At the opening of the play we find Strepsiades lying in bed, worrying about how to deal with his debts. By lines 136–52 he has decided to go to Socrates' school to learn the art of skillful speaking in order to evade the necessity of repaying his creditors. The rest of the play is about the education of Strepsiades and his son Pheidippides in the newly invented arts of sophistic rhetoric.

The character of Strepsiades has proven puzzling to critics. At certain points, he appears to be fairly shrewd, at least in terms of common sense, and at other points almost unbelievably dense. He seems on occasion to display an old-fashioned and upright set of ethical principles, and at other times to be quite unscrupulous. The only definite quality we can attribute to him throughout the play is that he is a rural character, who thinks in generally agricultural terms.

My own sense of Strepsiades perhaps evolves from my having lived for many years in the rural intermountain western United States, and actually having done much of the work on the translation while living in Montana— I think I am the only translator to have recognized line 51 as an innuendo about a possibly intimate relationship between Strepsiades and his ewes prior to his marriage, and to suspect that he recalls said intimacy with some degree of nostalgia. More important than any one specific joke is my sense of Strepsiades' overall attitude. I see him as a relatively shrewd farmer who distrusts "city slickers," with their fancy (and somewhat incomprehensible) habits of clothing, entertainment, and economic interactions. He expresses his distrust of "the suits in the city," as it were, by playing dumb, using his pose as a rural hick to express a heavily ironic disbelief in the absurd utterances of the Socratics and their followers. A typical example is his response to a student's account of Socrates' brilliance. The student boasts of the intellectual acumen of the Socratics by telling stories about Chairephon measuring how far a flea could jump, about Socrates determining whether a gnat whistles out of its mouth or its anus, and about Socrates stealing a cloak. To these Strepsiades responds: "And I used to be amazed at the tales about Thales!" (196). While this line is sometimes read as evidence of Strepsiades' credulity, I find it rather obviously sarcastic, the comment of a hard-headed farmer who thinks that spending one's days wondering about fleas' feet or gnats' anuses is utterly absurd. It also strikes me as similar, in a rather worrisome manner, to the comments by some members of the general public and the state legislature about the value of university education in general and the humanities (especially the postmodernist variants) in particular, that I see occasionally in my local newspaper, the *Bozeman Daily Chronicle*.

Strepsiades' attitude toward his creditors becomes comprehensible in light of a rural attitude toward economics that one sees not only in ancient Greece but also in many other farm communities including those in contemporary North America. Farmers are often suspicious of a cash and credit-based economy—Strepsiades' attitude toward cash and credit are not too far from those we find in Hesiod's *Works and Days* and Xenophon's *Oeconomicus* (which, like *Clouds*, includes Socrates as a major character). The economy that seems most real to the farmer is the barter one; cash comes second, and credit a distant third. The Midwestern farmers during the Depression and Dust Bowl whose farms were being repossessed by banks did not necessarily see the debts to banks as legitimate, but rather saw the bankers as people who did not work, and thus did not deserve, the land. Repayment of mortgages, many farmers felt, should vary with the success of the crops, not the whims of the banks, an attitude we see in Strepsiades when he is outraged at the unwillingness of his creditors to negotiate with him (1230–39), and claims that they, in fact, have been mistreating him.

Whether *Clouds* should be considered a pure comedy or a tragicomedy depends on the character of Strepsiades. If Strepsiades is indeed dishonest and unscrupulous, whether stupid or shrewd, a story that has him getting beaten and an equally unethical sophistic Socrates getting burned is a typical comedy, showing characters worse than the average human getting well deserved punishments. If, on the other hand, Strepsiades is basically a decent and sensible farmer in unfortunate circumstances due to the urbanization of Greek life, and Socrates an ethical, if slightly arcane and ineffectual, philosopher, then the play is a tragicomedy. I tend to favor the latter reading.

It seems to me that Strepsiades and Socrates have some similar values—thrift, conservative morality, and a preference for a barter over a cash economy. It is worth noting that Socrates never actually does accept money from Strepsiades, but instead takes "gifts" of clothing and food—like a typical comedic parasite, but also in the manner that Xenophon in *Oeconomicus* specifically shows his Socratic character as advocating for the livelihood of impoverished young gentlemen, who need to find some means of support without taking paid employment in a manner unacceptable to gentleman (*kaloi kagathoi*, a phrase also used to describe the Socratics by Strepsiades in line 110). Pheidippides, the Worse Argument, and the Creditors are the natural enemies of both Strepsiades and Socrates, the Chorus and the Better Argument their natural allies. Despite the obscene humor, the plot takes on the inexorable movement more typical to tragedy. Despite warnings from the Chorus (lines 480–530 are typically paradoxical—the Chorus can be interpreted as promising Strepsiades success or predicting his downfall) Strepsiades takes a course that leads inevitably to the downfall of the system he supports. The Aristophanic Socrates has the same effect on Pheidippides as the Platonic one had on Alcibiades or Critias or Callicles or Euthyphro—taking men suspicious of philosophy and leading them either to total rejection of philosophy or employment of dialectical tools for quite unphilosophical ends. *Clouds* seems a play suited to the Aristophanes of the Platonic *Symposium*, who tells a comic fable with serious import, and worries about not being taken seriously. Stylistically, *Clouds* is almost purely comedic, but its narrative and ethical message are tragic.

Even the bawdy jokes make a serious point about the implications of sexuality for the *polis*. The jokes about sexuality begin in a rather abstract fashion, with a discussion of grammatical gender (732ff.), which in the comments about Cleonymus immediately shifts from the linguistic realm of grammar to the ontological realm of appropriate masculine behavior. The breakdown of gender roles, symbolically in the case of grammar and realistically in the case of personal habits, results in the social problems. The Better Argument warns against the dangers of masturbation and effeminacy. In Strepsiades, whose old-fashioned education was unable to eradicate his natural proclivities for the habit, we see a preference for masturbation that might well account for his only having a single and rather unimpressive offspring. The Socratics and the Worse Argument seem to be characterized by habits of passive sodomy that lead to effeminacy. The types of men (and education in physical strength as well as responsibility) the Better Argument would say won the Battle of Marathon for Athens are scarce and not reproducing themselves. The city of Athens, which won the war against the Persians, is losing against the Spartans, and the alliance between the cleverness, thrift, and subtle ethics of the Socratics and the old-fashioned solidity and uprightness of the gentleman-farmers that could have restored Athens to her former glory has failed. The experiment of the Thinkateria and of Strepsiades' and Pheidippides' education therein has failed, and the building is consumed in a huge conflagration and its occupants burned or murdered, just like the occupants of a city which has failed to outlast a siege.

The satiric purpose of *Clouds* seems to me to be quite a serious one, to alert the Athenians to real and pressing dangers to their culture, both from external sources (the "nearness" of Sparta mentioned at line 232) and internal corruption. For the contemporary reader as well, *Clouds* can still be read as a cautionary tale about the relationship of ethics to education and the way in which their failure to work together can adversely affect a society.

Research for this translation was supported by a College of Liberal Arts and Sciences Research and Creativity grant from Montana State University and completed at the Bodleian Library, Oxford. An early version of this Introduction was first presented as a paper at the American Society for the History of Rhetoric Colloquium in San Diego, November 1996. I would like to extend thanks to Timothy Jane, Jeni Pearson, and especially Sara Jayne Steen, Chair of the Montana State University English Department. My greatest thanks go to John T. Kirby, for his many helpful comments.

BIBLIOGRAPHY

Major Editions, Translations, and Commentaries

Aristophanes. *Aristophanis Nubes* cum prolegomenis et commentariis edidit J. van Leeuwen. 2nd edition. 1898. Reprint Leiden: A. W. Sijthoff, 1968.

————. *The Clouds of Aristophanes*, with introduction, English prose translation, critical notes, and commentary, including a new transcript
of the scholia in the Codex Venetus Marcianus 474, by W. J. M.
Starkie. London: Macmillan, 1911. Reprint Amsterdam: Hakkert,
1966.

————. *The Clouds*. With translation, introduction, and commentary by
Benjamin Bickley Rogers. London: G. Bell and Sons, 1916.

————. *Clouds*. Edited with introduction and commentary by K. J. Dover.
Oxford: Clarendon Press, 1968.

————. *Clouds: English & Greek*. Edited with translation and notes by
Alan H. Sommerstein. Warminster, Wiltshire: Aris and Phillips,
1982.

Koster, W. J. W., edidit, varias lectiones adiecit, commentariis instruxit.
*Scholia in Aristophanus Plutum et Nubes vetera, Thomae Magistri,
Demetrii Triclinee nec non anonyma recentiora partim inedita*. Lug-
dune Batavorum: A. W. Sijtoff, 1927.

Selected Secondary Sources

Dover, Kenneth James. *Aristophanic Comedy*. Berkeley: University of California Press, 1972.

Henderson, Jeffrey. *The Maculate Muse: Obscene Language in Attic Comedy*.
New Haven, Conn.: Yale University Press, 1975.

Hubbard, Thomas K. *The Masks of Comedy: Aristophanes and the Intertextual Parabasis*. Ithaca, N.Y.: Cornell University Press, 1991.

MacDowell, Douglas M. *Aristophanes and Athens: An Introduction to the
Plays*. Oxford and New York: Oxford University Press, 1995.

Marianetti, Marie C. *Religion and Politics in Aristophanes' Clouds*. Hildes-
heim and New York: Olms-Weidmann, 1992.

O'Regan, Daphne Elizabeth. *Rhetoric, Comedy, and the Violence of Language
in Aristophanes' Clouds*. New York: Oxford University Press, 1992.

Reckford, Kenneth J. *Aristophanes' Old-and-New Comedy*. Chapel Hill: University of North Carolina Press, 1987.

Strauss, Leo. *Socrates and Aristophanes*. Chicago: University of Chicago
Press, 1980.

Cast

STREPSIADES, son of Pheidon, of Cicynna, a farmer wealthy in
   land but very short on cash
SLAVES of Strepsiades' household
PHEIDIPPIDES, son of Strepsiades and his aristocratic city wife
STUDENT 1 at the Thinkateria
SOCRATES, a philosopher
CHORUS of Clouds
BETTER ARGUMENT
WORSE ARGUMENT
FIRST CREDITOR
WITNESS, accompanies first creditor
SECOND CREDITOR
STUDENT 2
NONSPEAKING
   Slaves
   Students
   Live ducks, one male and one female

*(Backdrop is of two houses, Strepsiades' and the Thinkateria, both
   with usable doors. The only two items always needed on the set
   are a herm, a crude bust of the god Hermes mounted on a pillar,
   on one side of the stage, and a similar pillar, surmounted by a
   large pitcher painted in a stylized spiral pattern to represent a
   whirlwind, in front of the Thinkateria. It is unlikely that Greek
   productions attempted to sustain any particular degree of realism
   with respect to locale. Slaves [or grips] bring in or remove props
   as needed, e.g., beds and scientific instruments.*
*When lights come up, Pheidippides is sleeping in his bed, wrapped
   up in a mound of expensive blankets, while Strepsiades is lying
   awake in bed covered with a solid if slightly worn wool cloak.
   These beds, actually pallets on the floor or futons, may be inside
   Strepsiades' house with doors opened to reveal them, or just
   outside. As it is late night, the lights should be relatively dim,
   perhaps just a faint spotlight on Strepsiades.)*

STREPSIADES

King Zeus! the nights are endless. I'll never see the light of day.
Hours ago I should have heard the rooster crow,
but no. The only sounds I hear are snores from my lazy
household. I miss the good old days, before the war,
when a man could beat his slaves, and not worry about
them running away. Now they sleep all night,
rather than rising to work before first light.
And nothing wakes my stupid son, who farts around
with his horses, day and night, asleep or awake,
wrapped in fancy clothes or piles of mohair blankets.   10
Maybe I should try sleep, to snore in harmony with them,
but no. I'm being gnawed by debts. Expenses crawl
like bedbugs in my bed, and creditors are swilling my cash
like thirsty horses sucking water from a trough,
because of my son. He curls and oils his hair,
rides thoroughbreds, and drives a chariot and pair.
He's obsessed with horses, and I am plagued with debts.
It's twenty days past the new moon, and my monthly payments
                    are nearly due.

(to slave offstage)

Boy! light a lamp. Bring me the ledger so I can review
how much interest I owe, and to whom.   20

*(A slave enters with a lighted lamp; the spotlight on Strepsiades
                    brightens. The slave retreats to a dark corner.)*

It looks like twelve minas to Pasias. Twelve minas to Pasias?
                    What for?
Twelve minas for a gelded thoroughbred?
I wish I'd been gelded instead, before I bred
that son of mine. He's as worthless as he is extravagant.

PHEIDIPPIDES *(talking in his sleep)*

Philo, you cheater! Stay in your own lane.

STREPSIADES

That's my problem. He's ruining me.
He's always riding his horses, even in his dreams.

PHEIDIPPIDES

    How many more laps should the chariots drive?

STREPSIADES

    How much closer to bankruptcy have you driven me?

    Next on my list, after the debt to Pasias, is one to Amynias.   30

    For a chariot body and wheels, three minas.

PHEIDIPPIDES

    After you've warmed him down, lead him home.

STREPSIADES

    If I don't get my debts paid down,

    you won't have a home to lead him to.

(Pheidippides stretches, wakes.)

    I've missed so many payments, my creditors

    are threatening to sue.

PHEIDIPPIDES

    Father, what's been bugging you?

    You've been tossing and turning the whole night through.

STREPSIADES

    Those bloodsucking creditors are after my hide,

    infesting my sleep like fleas in my sheets.   40

PHEIDIPPIDES

    That's no reason to keep me awake.

(Pheidippides falls back asleep.)

STREPSIADES

    As you drift off to sleep, you forget,

    that my debts will be your entire inheritance.

    I wish I could find the matchmaker

    who set me up with your mother and make her suffer.

    I was a happy country boy, who didn't curl or comb his hair,

    covered with honest dirt and sweat, rather than expensive scents.

I made my own honey and cheese and olives,
rather than buying luxury foods and running into debt.
Instead of lying awake, worrying all night about getting sued,   50
I'd curl up and sleep under the stars with my ewes.
Then I married her, a niece of Megacles, son of Megacles,
a city girl, noble, sophisticated, and unbelievably extravagant.
She even smelled rich, as if she'd just returned
from Aphrodite's rituals, scented with incense,
perfumes, lotions, French kisses, and saffron silk.
And I was sleeping with her, a farmer, stinking
of rotgut wine and figs and goats and sour milk.
Like a good farmer's wife, she'd make her clothes,
but with gold thread and saffron-dyed cloth.   60
I lost money with every inch she wove.

SLAVE
The lamp is running out of oil.

STREPSIADES
Why did you use so thick a wick?
That sucker eats up oil faster than my son
drinks up imported wines.
                                   I'll get my whip.

SLAVE *(backing away)*
Why should I be whipped?
(Exit slave.)

STREPSIADES *(calling after him)*
Because you're burning up my money with your wick.
Then this son of ours was born,
to me, a poor farmer, and my stuck-up wife.
We fought about his name for days.   70
She held out for "hippo" (meaning "horse"),
but I wanted "Fido" (after my dog).
She said "Fido" sounded rude and coarse,

so we called him Pheidippides, a mix
between a stallion and a bitch.
She spoiled him rotten, always talking of the day
he'd ride a chariot in the Panathenaic parade,
wearing a swirling saffron cloak, just like hers,
or the generations of Megacles'.
Meanwhile, I talked of his driving flocks to summer pastures,   80
wearing a warm goatskin to ward off the cold, just like his father.
But he didn't listen. He was infected with a horse fever
so hot that it burned up all of my money.
(Strepsiades pauses, thinks, watches Pheidippides sleep.)
But after searching all night for a way around my dilemma,
I've got an idea—sneaky and almost inhumanly clever.
If I can persuade him to do what I say, I'll be saved.
But first I'll need to wake him gently, so he'll be
in the right mood to listen to me.
(whispers softly)
Pheidippides? Pheidippides? Fido?

PHEIDIPPIDES *(yawning)*

What, father?

STREPSIADES
Let me shake your hand and make a deal.   90
(They both get up.)

PHEIDIPPIDES
Done. What do you want?

STREPSIADES
Tell me, do you love your father?

PHEIDIPPIDES
Yes, I swear, by Poseidon, the god of horses,
whose statue I keep over there.

STREPSIADES

No! no! Not by him.
He's been the source of all my troubles. But if, my dearest son,
you love me from the bottom of your heart, obey me now, just
this once.

PHEIDIPPIDES

What do you want me to do?

STREPSIADES

You must turn away from your present course,
and learn the new ways I'll tell you about.

PHEIDIPPIDES

Whatever you say.

STREPSIADES

Promise me you'll obey?

PHEIDIPPIDES

By Dionysus
I'll obey.
*(Strepsiades walks Pheidippides a bit closer to Thinkateria door, followed
by spotlight. A slave removes the two beds as they
talk. Rest of lights begin to brighten very gradually,
to represent dawning of new day.)*

STREPSIADES

Pay attention.   100
Do you see the courtyard wall and little door over there?

PHEIDIPPIDES

Yes, father. I see it. So?

STREPSIADES *(pompously)*

That is the Thinkateria, home of the wise guys.
The men who live there have figured out the universe.

They say it's like a huge wood stove enclosing the world,
and we're like the embers burning inside.
                                    If I give them
a bunch of silver coins, they'll teach you to speak
so well you'll win any lawsuit brought against us,
whether just or unjust.

PHEIDIPPIDES

                    Who are they?

STREPSIADES

                        I don't know their true names,
but they're famous scholars, and gentlemen.   110

PHEIDIPPIDES

Bleech! You're talking about Socrates and Chairephon.
They're disgustingly ugly. Their bare feet are filthy
and their skin is paler than a bottom-feeding fish's underbelly.

STREPSIADES

Shut up! And stop whining like a baby.
Think of your poor aging father, barely able to afford a bowl of
                    porridge,
and abandon your expensive horses to enroll in their courses.

PHEIDIPPIDES

By Dionysus, not even if you gave me
a matched pair of the show horses Leogoras breeds.

STREPSIADES

I beg you, my dearest son, for my sake, go and let yourself
be taught.

PHEIDIPPIDES

                For your sake? What would I learn?   120

STREPSIADES

> I've heard that they claim to know two Arguments
> about everything, a better and a worse. It's this other,
> the worse, the latter of the Arguments, they say,
> that gives a man victory even in pleading an unjust case.
> I want you to learn the unjust kind of Argument,
> and talk me free of all my debts,
> so I won't need to repay a single cent.

PHEIDIPPIDES

> Forget it. After spending months indoors, growing flabby
>   and pale,
> I'd be ashamed to meet my friends, much less to enter a
>   horse race.

STREPSIADES

> By Demeter, if you disobey you'll never eat again at my table,   130
> much less have your quarter horses housed in my stable.
> You can go fight the crows for dinners of dead animals,
> and you can take your horses down to the knackers.

PHEIDIPPIDES

> My uncle Megacles would never let me go horseless;
> I'll go to his house, not to the Thinkateria.
> *(Exit Pheidippides.)*

STREPSIADES

> I'm down but not yet out. I won't give up.
> I'll pray to the gods to give me strength,
> and go to the Thinkateria myself.
> *(hesitating)*
> My problem is that I'm old, and a little slow,
> so how can I keep up with their quick-witted quibbling?   140
> Because I have no choice. I need to go,
> and stop dithering. I'll knock on the door.
> *(He knocks on the door of the Thinkateria.)*
>   Yo! Boy!

STUDENT 1 *(from indoors)*
> To hell with it.
(opening the door slightly)
>> Who's knocking at the door?

STREPSIADES
> Strepsiades of Cicynna, son of Pheidon.

STUDENT 1
> Goddammit, what kind of idiot can you be
> to come here kicking and pounding the door so violently?
> You made something I'd been laboring over for months miscarry.

STREPSIADES
> I'm sorry. I'm just a poor farmer from the country.
> Could you explain to me what I made miscarry?

STUDENT 1
> It's against our rules to tell outsiders   150
> the secrets of our school.

STREPSIADES
>> You can tell me everything.
> I plan to enroll as a student in your Thinkateria immediately.

STUDENT 1
> I'll tell you, if you'll promise to take my words seriously,
> and treat them, according to our rules, as sacred mysteries.
> Socrates just asked Chairephon to calculate
> how many times the length of its own feet a flea could leap,
> after one had just demonstrated its jumping prowess
> by leaping from Chairephon's bushy eyebrows
> to Socrates' bald spot.

STREPSIADES
>> How could he measure that?

STUDENT 1

> He was very clever. He dipped each   160
> of the flea's feet in melted wax to find its foot size.
> When the wax dried he removed it and used it
> as a mold to manufacture flea-foot sized measuring devices.
> Next time it jumped, he used these to pace off the distance.

STREPSIADES

> By King Zeus, what amazing insight!

STUDENT 1

> Would you like me to tell you another instance
> of Socrates' quasi-divine intelligence?

STREPSIADES

> Oh please! I beg you. Tell me!

STUDENT 1

> Chairephon of Sphettos asked him, once upon a time,
> which widely held piece of folk wisdom was right: 170
> do gnats whistle out of their mouths or their assholes?

STREPSIADES

> What sort of answer did he give?

STUDENT 1

> He answered that when a gnat exhales,
> because it has such a narrow nose,
> the air is forced back toward its asshole.
> The colon, being hollow, amplifies the sound,
> and so its whistle through its anus resounds.

STREPSIADES

> So the anus of a gnat is like a war-trumpet.
> What a wonderful piece of gnat-picking!

(aside)

> For someone who waxes so eloquent about a gnat's ass,   180
> it should be a piece of cake to help me escape my creditors.

STUDENT 1

Last night a momentous piece of wisdom went unrevealed
because a gecko intervened.

STREPSIADES

How? Could you explain it to me?

STUDENT 1

Socrates was gazing up at the roof,
investigating the paths by which the moon revolves,
when a gecko spattered him with excrement.

STREPSIADES

Socrates fouled by a lizard. I like that!

STUDENT 1

Let me tell you another story. We're so unpopular,
yesterday, we almost went without our dinner.

STREPSIADES

To get you your meal, did Socrates do something very clever?   190

STUDENT 1

We went down to the wrestling school,
and he sprinkled a layer of fine ashes on a brazier,
then used a bent skewer as a compass,
and as with one end of it he drew geometrical patterns,
with the other end he snitched a fancy cloak from one of the
                    patrons.

STREPSIADES

And I used to be amazed at the tales about Thales!
Hurry up and open the door! I want to enroll in the Thinkateria.
Quickly! Show me the way to Socrates!
*(The door opens, revealing a courtyard strewn with students hunched
                    over odd scientific instruments. If necessary these
                    students can be played by members of the chorus.*

> *Alternatively, the sights described can be offstage*
> *and indicated only by words. The precise staging of*
> *this scene will vary tremendously with the nature of*
> *the production. The ancient staging is uncertain.)*

Heracles! What sort of strange creatures are these?

STUDENT 1

Why are you so confused? What do they look like to you?   200

STREPSIADES

They look like the prisoners we dragged back from Pylos
in chains—the Spartans. Why are they staring at the earth?

STUDENT 1

They seek to unearth the mysteries of the ground.

STREPSIADES

I understand now. They're rooting for bulbs,
like onions and truffles and turnips. Tell them not to bother,
I know where the biggest and best ones can be found.
But why are they all bent over like hunchbacks?

STUDENT 1

They are searching for Tartarus under Erebos,
the very bottom of the underworld.

STREPSIADES

But why then do they point their asses to the sky,   210
unless they have their eyes (and brains) in their backsides?

STUDENT 1

So that they can learn the *assentials* of astronomy.
(to students)
Get inside. You don't want Him to see you exposed
to the great outdoors.
(Exit students, leaving their instruments behind.)

STREPSIADES

                        Not yet. Can't they stay a while
so I can explain my little problem to them?

STUDENT 1

They're not allowed to linger outside.
(walking toward door)

STREPSIADES

By the gods, tell me, what's that stuff for?

STUDENT 1

Astronomy.

STREPSIADES

          And those?

STUDENT 1

                   Geometry.

STREPSIADES

                          What does it do?

STUDENT 1

It helps us understand the true measure of the land.

STREPSIADES

You mean it helps you figure out water rights and grazing
                allotments . . .   220

STUDENT 1

No, not just that, the entire cosmos . . .

STREPSIADES

                        Oh, I see.
How slick. You work out homestead boundaries and government
                handouts
for people emigrating to the colonies. How useful for our
                democracy!

STUDENT 1

> Look. This is a map of the entire world. Here, for example,
> is Athens.

STREPSIADES

> It can't be. I don't see any lawsuits in progress or hung juries.

STUDENT 1

> This really is Attica, the entire county.

STREPSIADES

> Where is my home town, Cicynna?

STUDENT 1

> Over there. And here, you see, is Euboea,
> getting thinner as it stretches away from the shore.

STREPSIADES

> It was Pericles that thinned it out,
> with all his fancy building programs and his wars.   230
> But where is Sparta?

STUDENT 1

> Sparta? It's right here.

STREPSIADES

> Could you move it further away? That's much too near.

STUDENT 1

> That's not the sort of thing a map can do.

STREPSIADES

> So much the worse for you.
> *(A spotlight should come up gradually to reveal Socrates suspended in a*
> *basket above the stage.)*
> Who's that man suspended up there?

STUDENT 1

That's his very self.

STREPSIADES

Whose very self?

STUDENT 1

Socrates.

STREPSIADES

Socrates himself?
Then can you shout to him for me? Loudly?

STUDENT 1

Do your own shouting. I'm too busy
to waste my time in idle conversation.
(*Exit student. During the ensuing conversation, slaves unobtrusively
supply the bed, crown, and flour needed for the
initiation and remove the scientific instruments.*)

STREPSIADES

Socrates? . . . You up there with your head in the clouds! . . .
Socrates!

SOCRATES

Mortal creature on the ground, why do you call me?   240

STREPSIADES

First of all, I entreat you, can you tell me what you're doing?

SOCRATES

I move through the air and think upon the sun up here.

STREPSIADES

So from your basket can you talk down to the gods
that we earth-bound men look up to?

SOCRATES

Why shouldn't I
see the highest matters most clearly when suspended
above quotidian worries? Up here where the air is thinnest,
my ideas are most rarefied and subtlest. I breathe the truth.
Down on the ground the force of the earth traps my mind
and dampens my soul like bewildering wine.
Just as the watercress grows tallest if not drenched   250
in briny water, I speculate best
when elevated above common sense.

STREPSIADES *(aside)*

He's saying that if you think too much
even watercress juice will make you drunk.
(to Socrates)
Socrates, will you descend to me
to teach me the things I came here for?

SOCRATES

Why did you come here?

STREPSIADES

I want you to teach me how to speak.
I am besieged by debts, and interest, and creditors,
and on the verge of having my property seized.

SOCRATES

What caused your debts to grow so great?   260

STREPSIADES

A plague of horses infected all my assets, a parasite
that inflates my debts as it shrinks my estate.
I want you to teach me the other Argument, the one
that enables me to evade my payments.
I'll give you a deposit and swear by the gods
to give you the balance as soon as I can.

SOCRATES

What sort of gods do you use as collateral?
We don't consider them as good as cash.

STREPSIADES

What do you swear by?
Iron? Like the Byzantines?

SOCRATES

Would you like to understand
holy things more clearly?

STREPSIADES

Yes, by Zeus, if I can.   270

SOCRATES

To have verbal intercourse with our goddesses,
the Clouds?

STREPSIADES

Yes, I would.

SOCRATES

Sit now on this holy bed.

STREPSIADES

I'm seated.

SOCRATES

Now take this crown . . .

STREPSIADES

Why
should I be garlanded like a victim for a sacrifice?

SOCRATES

Not a victim but an initiate.

STREPSIADES

And what do I gain from it?

SOCRATES *(sprinkling Strepsiades with flour)*
You'll become a nimble speaker, an agile thinker,
words will rattle off your tongue like thunder from a kettle drum,
your thoughts will be finely sifted . . . Stop twitching!

STREPSIADES
By Zeus, no false accusations will ever stick to me,
my briefs are becoming so floury.   280

SOCRATES
Old man, you must strive for a reverent silence,
and listen attentively to our sacred invocations.
O Lord of Lords, boundless Air, you who surround
        heaven and earth, sky and ground,
brilliant Aether, and most revered Goddesses,
        Clouds who send thunder, ascend,
shine forth your glories, divinest of Ladies,
        elevate this wisdom-seeker.

STREPSIADES
Not yet, not yet! Wait until I wrap my cloak over my head.
I didn't even bring a leather rain cap from my house; I'll be
        drenched.   290

SOCRATES
Awe-inspiring Clouds,
        show yourselves, come here now.
Whether you are seated on the holy reaches
        of snow-capped Olympus,
or you stay in your father Ocean's garden,
        performing holy dances for the Nymphs,
or you draw up golden waters from the Nile delta,
        to pour them forth again as life-giving rain,

or whether you linger above the marshy sea of Azov,
    on the snowy peaks of Mimas Mountain,   300
answer these sacred rites, receive these holy offerings,
    greet your acolytes.

(Enter Chorus of Clouds, gradually, through the aisles of the audience,
        where Strepsiades, especially if grown slightly
        shortsighted in his old age, might not be able to
        see them easily.)

CHORUS
    We, the eternal Clouds, arise,
    our watery nature undefiled,
    from Father Ocean's murky depths
    to the mountains' lofty summits,
    overgrown with towering trees,
    from where, spread out beneath us, we can see
    the fertile lands of the earth goddess,
    the spirits of the rushing rivers,   310
    roaring waves, and crashing seas.
    The unsleeping eyes of the Aether
    sparkle in the sun's first rays,
    chasing away the clouds and rain,
    so we can watch the deathless forms
    or with immortal eyes look down
    on the mortal world.

(Loud roll of thunder.)

SOCRATES
    O great Clouds, most revered Ladies, you have appeared,
    your divine fear-inspiring thunder answered my prayers.

STREPSIADES
    I am quaking with fear so badly I feel ready to fart loudly   320
    in harmony with their rumbling. My stomach churns in terror.
    And if they won't permit a fart, I'll let loose a load of excrement.

SOCRATES

This is no time for you to joke like a vulgar comedian,
the great swarm of goddesses are about to start singing.
Maintain a respectful silence in their presence.

CHORUS

We come to the land of Pallas,
its fertile earth gleaming with groves of olives,
tended by men known for their goodness,
ourselves, like Athena, virgin goddesses,
bringers of rain, filled with benevolence.   330
We come to the land that celebrates
the ineffable mysteries, the rites of the grain,
where the blessed dwelling is dedicated
to the holy initiates being consecrated,
a place where gifts for the heavenly gods are displayed
in high-vaulted treasuries decorated
with statues and precious inlays,
their entrances blessed with sacred offerings,
of all the holy days, visited by the Graces,
filled with the sounds of music contests,   340
and the sights of the ritual dances,
and a magical blending of flute song and incense.

STREPSIADES

By Zeus, I beg you, Socrates, could you tell me, who are those
                    ladies,
speaking so loudly and so solemnly? Are they heroines out of
                    some ancient story?

SOCRATES

No. They are the heavenly Clouds, the ideal goddesses for
                    lazy men.
If you want cleverness and logic-chopping and impressive
                    maxims, listen to them.
They provide circumlocutions and tall tales, strategic deceptions
                    and dazzling defenses,

brilliant prosecutions and confusing claims, to cloud the minds
of all your opponents.

STREPSIADES

When I heard their voices my soul quivered like a hound on a
leash,
straining to chase after sententious sayings and luminous
legalities and sneaky subtleties   350
and to follow frivolous fancies and unfair judgments, by
mastering the other Argument.
If it's not forbidden, I'd like to see them.

SOCRATES

Look over there toward the mountains,
where they descend in utter silence.

STREPSIADES

Tell me, where? Show them to me!

SOCRATES

A host of clouds spread through the hollows and crown the
copses,
blown by the wind.

STREPSIADES

What's the problem? Why can't I see them?

SOCRATES

Look in the aisles, by the entrance.

STREPSIADES

There they are. I can just barely make them out.

SOCRATES

They should be clear to you now, unless your eyes are as blind
as a potato's.

STREPSIADES

By Zeus, I see their imposing forms approaching now,
expanding to fill everything.   360

SOCRATES

Have you just become aware of their divinity?

STREPSIADES

By Zeus, I used to think that they were just made of fog and dew,
as insubstantial as smoke or shadows.

SOCRATES

Not by Zeus at all. The Clouds cultivate
the greatest sophists and medical theorists and multicultural
                    sophisticates,
(like the Thurii's inhabitants), and their most extravagantly
                    useless
hangers-on, and writers of bombastic dithyrambs, and exotic
                    dancers,
and men with highbrow reputations. They don't associate with
                    men of action,
but with poets who live by telling stories about other men's
                    glories.

STREPSIADES

That's why those poetic parasites write: 370

      "Moist Clouds, like a braided bracelet coiling . . ."
      or "Clouds, like the curling hair of the hundred-headed
                    Typhos . . ."

or even:

      "They clasp the crags with dewy hands
      close to the sun in lonely lands,
      ring'd with the azure world they stand.

The wrinkled sea beneath them crawls,
they look down from their mountain walls,
and cause the thunderbolts to fall.''

And in return for this feast of words, the poets are invited to
        gorge   380
on banquets of mullet and steak and game birds and
        gourmet food.

SOCRATES
    And don't they deserve it?

STREPSIADES
                Tell me, please, what is the reason
these Clouds now look just like an ordinary chorus of mortal
        women?
(points at the chorus)

SOCRATES
    Tell me, what do normal clouds appear to be?
*(He points up at real clouds or, in an indoor theater, scenery painted to
        resemble clouds.)*

STREPSIADES
    I can't see them clearly, but they look like puffy cotton sails
        spread out to dry,
and not like women. By Zeus, even seen up close, they wouldn't
        have noses.

SOCRATES
    Now can you answer another question?

STREPSIADES
                Any one you pose.

SOCRATES

Have you ever seen clouds form the shape of an animal—
a centaur, a leopard, a wolf, or even a bull?

STREPSIADES

Yes, by Zeus. So?

SOCRATES

They can become whatever they want. When they see some
shaggy savage,   390
like Xenophantes' son, or hear his ravings, they mock him with
a centaur's shape,
beasts almost as active pederasts as he is.

STREPSIADES

And what do they do when they watch
Simon who always has his snout in the public trough?

SOCRATES

They become hogs.

STREPSIADES

That's why they looked like startled deer the other day.
They must have glimpsed that fat coward Cleonymus,
who drops his shield and runs away at the first sight of the
enemy.

SOCRATES

And Kleisthenes is so effeminate that when they saw him
they assumed the forms of mortal women.

STREPSIADES

Greeting, heavenly ladies, Queens of all you see,
could you raise your voices and speak to me?   400

CHORUS

> Greetings, old man, born in better times, who now eagerly
>> pursues
> art and logic and eloquence. And greetings to you, Socrates, high
>> priest
> of logic puzzles and trivia contests. Tell us what you want
>> from us.
> We listen more closely to you than to any of the other highbrow
>> sophists,
> except for Prodicus, whose collection of useless facts and obscure
>> quotations
> is unsurpassed. But you are just our type, with your sideways
>> leering glances
> and dirty bare feet, pompous manner and grave face, and
>> devotion to our ways.

STREPSIADES

> By Gaia! How holy and miraculous are their solemn intonations.

SOCRATES

> They are the only true goddesses; the others are useless
>> imitations.

STREPSIADES

> By Zeus, come on, you can't mean that the Olympians aren't
>> gods to you!   410

SOCRATES

> What Zeus? Don't talk nonsense. Zeus doesn't even exist.

STREPSIADES

>   How can that be?
> Without Zeus, how can you explain what makes it rain?

SOCRATES

>I can teach you why by means of the signs in the sky.
>Look. Have you ever seen it rain on a cloudless day?
>To prove that Clouds cause rain, all I need to point out
>is that you'll never see a raindrop without them.

STREPSIADES

>By Apollo, I'm convinced. I used to believe that water
>falling from heaven was caused by Zeus' golden showers
>strained through a sieve into tiny droplets, but now
>you've argued so well that I know better.   420
>Now tell me the cause of the thunder that makes me quake and
>   shudder?

SOCRATES

>Thunder resounds when the Clouds whirl around.

STREPSIADES

>   How?

SOCRATES

>The Clouds by their nature are compelled to carry
>raindrops in their bellies. When they are swollen with moisture
>   they rush
>across the heavens, splashing and groaning, until they explode in
>   a flood of water.

STREPSIADES

>What is this Nature that compels them? Is it not Zeus himself?

SOCRATES

>Of course not. It's a whirlwind of swirling air.

STREPSIADES

>   Whirlwind? The news hadn't reached me
>that it wasn't Zeus any longer but Whirlwind who was the King.

But that tells me nothing about the crashing thunder. Can you
        explain it?

SOCRATES
    Didn't you listen to what I said? If the Clouds are filled with
            water,   430
    they're so dense that when they collide they clash and rumble and
            thunder.

STREPSIADES
    Come on, who could believe that stuff?

SOCRATES
                    I'll make it simple by using you as an example.
    Have you ever stuffed yourself with bean and sausage soup at a
            festival,
    and when you got up and started to move, your bowels suddenly
            began to rumble?

STREPSIADES
    By Apollo, yes. It starts out softly, shaking and grumbling,
        sounding like this,
    (imitates farting noise)
                    and then it gets louder,
    (repeats the same noise, but considerably louder and longer)
        and when I finally drop my load, it goes like this:
    (imitates same noise at maximum intensity)
                        just like the Clouds when they thunder.

SOCRATES
    Now consider the small size of the stomach from which you fart.
    Since the heavens are so much larger, is it not probable they'll
            rumble louder?
    This similarity is why you say you're scared shitless when it
            thunders.   440

STREPSIADES

But what about lightning? Teach me how they produce those
                    flaming bolts,
scorching everything they strike, sometimes burning us to ashes,
sometimes leaving us alive. Isn't this how Zeus punishes perjury?

SOCRATES *(aside)*

This moron's so old, he's almost completely covered with mold.
(to Strepsiades)

If Zeus hurled his thunderbolts at all the perjurers,
then why wasn't Simon the Sophist consumed by flames,
or the cowardly Cleonymus made to quake,
or Theorus blasted for his freeloading habits?
But instead the bolts rained down on Sunion, the holy
                    promontory,
and shattered the great oaks. Why? Surely the trees had broken
                    no oaths.   450

STREPSIADES

I don't know. You have some good arguments. Then what is it?

SOCRATES

When the dry wind whirling high into the Clouds,
constrained by the lightness of its nature,
fills them up as if they were bladders, and stretches them taut,
they explode and the hot air pours out in flaming bolts.

STREPSIADES

By Zeus, something like that happened to me once at Zeus'
                    Festival,
the first time I cooked a haggis for my family. I get distracted for
                    a bit,
and suddenly it burst, and spattered like piss, and spit fat at
                    my face,
and singed my eyebrows and just missed my eyes by an inch.

CHORUS

> If a man yearns with all his heart to learn wisdom from us,   460
> and earn more wealth than the Athenians and everyone else,
> he must possess good memory, determination, and native
>> intelligence.
> He won't complain when his progress slows or stops entirely,
> nor slack off when things seem hopeless. He'll avoid the
>> best wines
> and abstain from the gymnasium and other mindless
>> occupations.
> This is how our shrewdest followers live. If you think our
>> way best,
> we can give you the skills to win your way in legislative
>> deliberation
> and overcome your opponents in all the battles of the tongues.

STREPSIADES

> I'm rugged enough, and definitely used to sleeping rough.
> I'm accustomed to thrift and hunger and pains in my stomach   470
> and eating boiled greens, so take me to mold as you please.

SOCRATES

> From now on you must believe that of the gods there are only
>> three:
> Chaos, Clouds, and the Tongues, who are sometimes called
>> Language.

STREPSIADES

> Even if one of the others tried to speak to me, or ran into me on
>> the street,
> I wouldn't burn incense or pour a libation or anything else.

CHORUS

> Say to us now what you wish us to do, and we will not fail you,
> if you live as a wise and steadfast and reverent man.

STREPSIADES

Oh Goddesses, I want from you only one very small favor:
of all the men in Greece I want to be by far the best speaker.

CHORUS

We can grant you this. No matter how many decrees you
                propose,   480
you'll never be outvoted. No one's laws will be more popular
                than yours.

STREPSIADES

Don't speak to me of major legislation; I don't want to rule our
                nation.
I just want to escape my creditors by twisting justice around
                a bit.

CHORUS

Since great deeds are not what you desire,
we'll give you the things to which you aspire.
Turn yourself over entirely to our followers without reservations.

STREPSIADES

I will, and I will obey them. I have no choice;
I'm stuck with thoroughbred horses and an expensive wife.
I'll yield myself to them completely,
both mind and body,   490
whether they want to beat me or starve me or make me go thirsty
or go unwashed or shiver with cold, however they want to
                mistreat me,
if only I can flee my debts and seem to be
confident and adventurous and eloquent and reckless,
a fearless fabricator of falsifications,
an inventor of arguments and evader of judgments,
a quibbling lawyer, a slick speaker and foxy fleecer,
an oily imposter and subtle dissembler,
a tricky troublemaker and branded felon,

a con man and convincing talker.   500
I won't care if I've won a bad reputation
or if my name is disgraced,
so long as my debts are evaded.
By Demeter, the Thinkateriasts can do
whatever they wish with me,
even make my guts into a tripe stew.

CHORUS *(to audience)*
He's certainly determined on this course,
without a trace
of cowardice or hesitation.
(to Strepsiades)
Realize that once   510
you have learned
      these arts from us,
your fame will spread across
      the mortal world
and even to the heavens.

STREPSIADES
Command me and I'll obey.

CHORUS
You must promise in perpetuity
      to spend your life with us,
devoting yourself
      to your studies   520
zealously.

STREPSIADES
Then what will happen to me?

CHORUS
Hordes of men will besiege your doors,
wanting to talk with you about the law courts,

about suits and countersuits and legal defenses,
about the huge sums of money appropriate
to your skills and intelligence.

(to audience)

But now, we'll hand over this old man to Socrates for
preliminary instruction,
to give him puzzles and tests and determine the extent of his
learning and his abilities.

SOCRATES

I'll need to measure your attainments and learning habits,   530
so I can target you with our newest and aptest educational
devices.

STREPSIADES

By the gods, I wonder what sort of shots he'll take at me.

SOCRATES

None. But I want you to supply some information for me.
What kind of memory do you have for tiny details?

STREPSIADES

I have two types:
if I'm owed any money, I remember each penny,
but if I'm in debt, I worry so much I forget it completely.

SOCRATES

Next, how good is your natural speaking ability?

STREPSIADES

Terrible, but I think I could manage to cheat quite easily.

SOCRATES

How will I be able to teach you, then?

STREPSIADES

Well, of course.   540

SOCRATES
> Follow me carefully. Whenever I toss out some profound
> > thought
> about the heavens, you must grab on to it quickly.

STREPSIADES
> Should I fetch and gnaw your thoughts like a hungry dog?

SOCRATES *(aside)*
> This man is an ignorant barbarian. I'm afraid he'll need a
> > beating.

(to Strepsiades)
> What would happen if someone beat you?

STREPSIADES
> > > > I'd be beaten, of course.
> *(He pauses while Socrates waits for him to elaborate.)*
> And then I'd wait a while, and look for witnesses,
> and after a bit I'd go to court and plead my case.

SOCRATES
> Now, take off your cloak.

STREPSIADES
> > > Do you intend to tan my hide?

SOCRATES
> It's our custom to take away most of your clothes before you go
> > inside.

STREPSIADES
> But I have nothing to hide.

SOCRATES
> > > Stop babbling and take it off.   550

STREPSIADES

    Can you answer one question first? If I devote myself zealously to
           my work,
    what sort of student will I become?

SOCRATES

    You'll follow in the footsteps of Chairephon.

STREPSIADES

    I've seen corpses looking better than him. I'm doomed.

SOCRATES

    Stop chattering and follow me.
    (Strepsiades starts to remove the cloak.)
    Hurry up! Quickly!
    (Strepsiades hangs back, peering into the door.)

STREPSIADES

    It's like descending to Trophonius' oracle,
    a vast cave guarded by a hungry snake.
    To ensure my safety, could you give me a honeycake?

SOCRATES

    Don't hesitate. Just stop peering and prying and go inside.   560
*(Strepsiades drops his cloak at the door and reluctantly follows Socrates
               into the Thinkateria, perhaps even being dragged
               by his arm or robe. When the chorus turns to face
               the audience, a student sneaks outside, peers
               around to make sure no one is watching, grabs the
               cloak, and then goes back inside, closing the door.)*

CHORUS *(to Strepsiades)*

    Goodbye. And go with our best wishes.
    May you be rewarded suitably for the courage you've shown.
    (all together)
    This old man seeks wisdom late in life.
    He follows a course appropriate

to younger minds and natures,
striving to learn the newest ideas
as his years wind down toward their finish.

(*Parabasis. The chorus turns to address the audience directly. In this
    section the chorus speaks in the first person in the voice of the
    playwright himself.*)

CHORUS LEADER
Spectators, I'm going to talk to you freely and openly and
                directly,
I swear, by Dionysus, who nourished and reared me.
First, I want to win this dramatic contest. It's no secret.   570
You're a good audience, or at least I thought so,
when I brought the first version of this play before you.
Of all my plays, this was the smartest and most serious,
and the most work, so I thought I'd show it to you first.
Then, this play, (the earlier version, that is), was defeated
by a coarse, crude, vulgar, simpleminded piece of slapstick.
I don't blame the wise ones among you for this.
Instead, I revised it, not for the rest of them, but for you, now,
because no matter how badly *they* misjudged me, I wouldn't let
                you down.
I've always enjoyed my audiences at this theater.   580
When I was too young to produce dramas for myself, my play,
The Lewd and the Chaste, was produced at a contest here.
The orphan drama I'd abandoned because of my age,
another man raised as his own, and it was awarded first place.
You helped him rear it; you taught and nourished and cared
                for it.
I took your good treatment of my first work as a promise of
                future charity.
Now, like the heroine Electra, this old and new comedy
seeks spectators as wise as you once appeared to me,
and will recognize them immediately, like the maiden on first
                seeing
her brother's hair. You will see the play's nature quite clearly,   590
in the beginning, wise and chaste, as when it was first produced,

no actors going round with huge leather phalluses hanging down
with bright red tips fit only to make kids snicker,
nor jokes about balding heads, nor obscene cordax dances,
nor old men flailing their canes at everyone who passes
to hide the weaknesses of their lines,
nor torches nor bonfires nor moans nor cries,
but lines that rely on their own devices,
by a genuine poet, not a long-haired imposter
trying to impress you with foolish excesses.   600
I won't try to cheat you with the same play, presented again and
                again,
but each drama I produce will introduce fresh plots and
                innovative humor;
no two will resemble each other, but all will be equally clever.
When Cleon was at the height of his fame, I attacked him
                without restraint,
but I won't mention him now, because I refuse to kick a man
                when he's down.
Other writers have just latched on to Hyperbolus and can make
                fun of no one else.
They've even dragged in his moneylending mother, kicking
                below the belt.
First Eupolis parodied Hyperbolus in his *Maricus*—
taking lines from my *Knights* and getting them wrong—
and making Hyperbolus' mother dance and sing a drunken song. 610
Then Phrynicus turned her into Andromache and had her eaten
                by monsters of the sea.
Next, Hermippus and his hangers-on joined in,
stealing my joke about how politicians were like fisherman,
stirring up mud to catch their eels.
If you enjoy plays like that, keep away from mine.
But if you appreciate me and like works like these,
posterity will think you very wise.

CHORUS
Great Zeus, who rules both gods and men,
to you we dedicate this dance.

We praise the greatest of the gods   620
and his trident-wielding brother,
king over earth and briny sea,
who shakes the ground and lashes the water
into ship-destroying waves,
our father, famous from earth to heaven,
the glorious Poseidon.

We also sing of Aether, bright
and shining, giver of life,
and Phoebus, the charioteer whose rays
warm ground and ocean, great among   630
divine spirits and gods and mortals.

Wisest of audiences, pay close attention to what we're about
                    to say.
You've been treating us unjustly for years, and now it's time to
                    confront you,
laying blame where it is due.
We've given more help to your city than any of the gods ever has,
but we're the only divinities to whom you give neither sacrifices
                    nor libations,
no matter how carefully we watch over you.
If your counsel proposes some reckless military expedition,
we thunder and drizzle to stop the vote,
and when you made the mistake of electing as your general   640
that disgusting Paphloginian, the hateful hide-tanner,
we sent down lightening bolts and roared and thundered,
and concealed the sun and moon for weeks,
and damped their lights almost to extinction,
until the Sun threatened to turn round his chariot,
But you elected Cleon despite this.
It is said that Poseidon cursed Athens with folly,
and since the gods cannot undo their words,
Pallas added that whenever you went wrong,
she'd cause you to turn things around, exchanging bad for good. 650
And so, we'll show you how to profit from Cleon's generalship:

indict Cleon the Magpie for fraud and for taking bribes,
and place his neck in a pillory
as you did to the criminals in the good old days,
and all will turn out for the best for your city.

Be with us Phoebus, Lord of Delos
    of high-peaked Mt. Cynthos,
and also your blessed sister,
    Artemis, Lady of Ephesus,
where Lydian girls worship   660
    in gilded temples,
and our native Athena,
    aegis-wielder,
our city's protector,
and you who light
    Parnassian ridges at night
with the sparkling torches
    of Bacchic rites,
god renowned for your revels,
    glorious Dionysus.   670

As we were preparing to travel here, we met the Moon goddess,
and she gave us an important message.
First she sent greetings, both to the Athenians and their allies.
Next, she said she was angry, because you had treated her badly,
although she's served you well, and not just with empty promises.
To begin with, she saves you a drachma each month in firewood.
Each of you has probably said to a slave before going out some
            evening:
"Don't chop wood for torches tonight; the full moon gives plenty
            of light."
Next she said, "I've done many other good deeds, but still you
            don't respect me.
Instead of organizing the calendar correctly, following my lead, 680
you rearrange it haphazardly, making the rest of the gods angry.
And when they're cheated of their sacrificial meals and return
            home empty,

they blame me.
Whenever you're supposed to be making sacrifices on
        festival days,
you're busy in the courts suing each other and torturing
        witnesses
and sitting on juries.
And when we are fasting, mourning Memnon and Sarpedon,
you're pouring libations and rejoicing, following your clever new
        calendars.
Recently, at the autumn meeting of the Amphictionic council,
Hyperbolus had the honor of acting as sacred recorder,   690
but he had disobeyed the gods, and by our will, his holy crown
was blown off onto the ground.
Let this be a warning to him and you,
live your life by the rules of the Moon.
(Enter Socrates.)

SOCRATES
    By Breath, by Chaos, and by Air,
    I've never seen such an idiot anywhere.
    He's clumsy and forgetful and scatterbrained,
    the slowest learner I've ever seen.
    If he manages to understand some minor point,
    it's forgotten almost before he's learned it.   700
    All the same, I'll call him out of doors into the sunlight.
    Strepsiades, where are you? Come out here, bringing your
        bedroll.

STREPSIADES *(from indoors)*
    But the bugs won't let me.

SOCRATES
    Hurry up.
(Enter Strepsiades, cloakless and barefoot, his robe looking a bit the worse
        for wear. He carries a bedroll consisting of several
        dirty sheepskins for a few feet, stops, drops it, swats
        at some of the bugs that are biting him. Since the

*bedroll has fallen open, he needs to reroll it, pick it
up again, drop it, swat more bugs, etc.)*

SOCRATES
Just leave it anywhere. Let's get back to work on wisdom.

STREPSIADES
                                                Whatever.

SOCRATES
Now what specific material should we cover first,
that you have not already learned? Metrics, rhythm,
or the correct use of words?

STREPSIADES
                        Meters.
Because recently a barley dealer cheated me by a liter.

SOCRATES
No, that wasn't what I asked. I meant, which do you consider   710
the most beautiful meter, the trimeter or the tetrameter?

STREPSIADES
As far as I'm concerned, the fairest measure of them all
is the one that makes the dealer pay me what I am owed.

SOCRATES
You're talking nonsense.

STREPSIADES
                    No, I'll wager
twelve liters against your baker's dozen I'm not.

SOCRATES
To hell with it. What you could learn the easiest
is how to become a village idiot.
But perhaps you'll be quicker at rhythms.

STREPSIADES

How can rhythms help me get paid for my barley?

SOCRATES

If you want to associate with educated men,   720
you'll need to appreciate the nuances of musical rhythm,
how to beat out time with wars drums or finger cymbals.

STREPSIADES

How to beat off with my fingers? By Zeus, I know that.

SOCRATES

Tell me about it.

STREPSIADES

I'd suck my thumb as a little boy,
but when I grew older I discovered a bigger toy.

SOCRATES

He's even dumber than he is vulgar.

STREPSIADES

You don't get it. I'm not interested in studying trivia.

SOCRATES

Then what is it you want?

STREPSIADES

What I told you before. To learn the Unjust Argument.   730

SOCRATES

First you need to learn the preliminaries.
Now, can you tell me which of the quadruped names are male?

STREPSIADES

Any sane man could name off some animals,
and half of all of them are male . . .
ram, boar, bull, dog, sheep, duck . . .

SOCRATES

>Now don't you see what you've just done?
>You're using the same words for male and female.

STREPSIADES

>What's wrong?

SOCRATES

>   Wrong? Duck and duck.

STREPSIADES

>By Poseidon, that even makes sense. What should I call them
>   instead?

SOCRATES

>Call one a ducker and the other a duckess.   740

STREPSIADES

>A duckess? By the (hot) Air, that's impressive.
>In return for that lesson alone you deserve
>your bread-making trough filled to the top with barley.

SOCRATES

>You've just made the same mistake again.
>You've assigned the trough to a male,
>though kneading dough is properly a woman's domain.

STREPSIADES

>And how do I make the trough feminine?

SOCRATES

>Think of Cleonymus.

STREPSIADES

>But Cleonymus doesn't have a wife or a trough for making bread.
>The only thing that gets kneaded in his house is himself.   750

Are you suggesting that since he's so effeminate,
I should call the trough Cleonymus?

SOCRATES
The proper feminine form is troughess.

STREPSIADES
Then I should call him Cleony*miss*.

SOCRATES
There's more you need to know about names.
As well as the males, you need to learn about the females.

STREPSIADES
I know plenty about them.

SOCRATES

Tell me some.

STREPSIADES *(lists off lasciviously the names of several famous prostitutes)*
Well, there are Aspasia's girls: Lucilla, Philinna, Kleitagora,
Demetria . . .

SOCRATES
Now what about some examples of the males?

STREPSIADES *(thinks of males engaged in approximately the same profession)*
Philoxenus, Melsias, Amynias . . .   760

SOCRATES
You worthless idiot. Those are not masculine.

STREPSIADES
They're not masculine?

SOCRATES

Not a bit. Tell me,
If you wrote a letter to Amynias, how would you address him?

STREPSIADES

How? "Dear Amynias . . ."

SOCRATES

And if you wrote to one of the women?

STREPSIADES

I'd start with "Dear . . ."

SOCRATES

You see, you address Amynias just like a woman.

STREPSIADES

That makes perfect sense. *She*'s such a coward,
she evaded her military service in the last war.
But why should I learn these things that everyone knows?

SOCRATES

By Zeus, never mind. Just get into the bed here.

STREPSIADES

And what do you want me to do in there?   770

SOCRATES

Think carefully over your affairs.

STREPSIADES

Please, I beg you, not in there. If I must,
I can work these things out on the bare ground.

SOCRATES

It is our custom to do it like this.

STREPSIADES

What bad luck!
For the sake of this custom, to be eaten by bugs.
(Socrates wanders off downstage in deep contemplation while Strepsiades talks with the chorus.)

CHORUS

You need to know yourself as well as you can.
Examine everything. Twist it and turn it, and if nothing happens,
come at it from a different angle again, not letting sweet sleep
divert you from your purpose.
(Strepsiades, taking their instructions perhaps overly literally, begins to masturbate.)

STREPSIADES

Ow! Ow!

CHORUS

What's the problem? Does something ache? 780

STREPSIADES

I'm in misery. The bugs are creeping out of the bedclothes and
biting me.
They gnaw on my ribs and nibble my testicles,
bore through my anus and drain my breath away.
I'm dying bit by bit.

CHORUS

Don't despair; many have suffered through worse than this and
lived.

STREPSIADES

I've lost my shoes and my health,
my skin and my wealth,
and worse, I'm nearly being bored to death.

And if I stay here longer and the bugs keep gnawing
I'll be eaten away to nothing.   790
(After a few seconds of silence Strepsiades returns to his usual means
of alleviating boredom—masturbation. Socrates
turns around and notices this. Strepsiades keeps
it up, as it were, through much of the ensuing
dialogue—to line 816.)

SOCRATES
What are you doing there? Are you thinking?

STREPSIADES
                                                        Me?
By Poseidon, yes.

SOCRATES
And what have you been contemplating?

STREPSIADES
Whether the bugs will leave any part of me uneaten.
(Strepsiades checks the part he's most concerned about.)

SOCRATES
Put that damn thing away.
(Socrates wanders off again.)

CHORUS
Just cover yourself up and concentrate.
Try to find some clever devices for dealing with fraud and
cheating.

STREPSIADES
Can sheepskins teach me how to cheat? Or only how to get
fleeced?
(Socrates turns around again.)

SOCRATES
>Come on, now, let me see how you're doing. Are you screwing
>>off again?

STREPSIADES
>By Apollo, certainly not.

SOCRATES
>>>What have you come up with?   800

STREPSIADES
>By Zeus, nothing yet.

SOCRATES
>>Nothing at all?

STREPSIADES *(pulling down covers to demonstrate his point)*
>Nothing except my penis in my right hand.

SOCRATES
>Just put that back under the covers. Now what are you thinking
>>about?

STREPSIADES
>About what? You show me yours first, Socrates.

SOCRATES
>What is it you want to find out?

STREPSIADES *(throwing back the covers again)*
>I've told you ten thousand times what I'm here for,
>to find out a way to avoid repaying my creditors.

SOCRATES
>Come on now, just cover that up again and let go.
>Now, think about your problems from a new direction.

Try a solution that's completely different,   810
clever and precise, and separated into its proper components.

STREPSIADES

How unfortunate I am.

SOCRATES
Stop twitching! If you come to a dead end, abandon it,
let go of that specific thought and come back to the
                    problem again
in a different way.
(*Socrates walks away.*)

STREPSIADES
Socrates, my dearest friend.

SOCRATES

What now, old man?

STREPSIADES
I have thought of a way to wriggle away from my debts.

SOCRATES
Let me see.
(*Strepsiades gets out of bed and inadvertently exposes himself again.*)

STREPSIADES

Now tell me . . .

SOCRATES

What's *that*?

STREPSIADES (*rearranging his robe more discreetly*)
If I hired a Thessalian woman who practiced sorcery,
one night I could have her capture the moon for me
and keep it safe in a helmet case.

SOCRATES

And how would that help you?   820

STREPSIADES

Because if the moon would never rise up again,
I wouldn't need to pay off my debts.

SOCRATES

Why not?

STREPSIADES

Because they're *monthly* payments.

SOCRATES

Very good. Now here's another tricky puzzle for you.
If someone brought a lawsuit against you for five talents,
how would you manage to wipe it out?

STREPSIADES

How? How? I don't know. Let me think.

SOCRATES

Don't tie yourself up into knots by trying too hard,
but slack off briefly and let your mind soar freely
like a kite released to soar through the air.   830

STREPSIADES

I've found the smartest way to obliterate the lawsuit.
I'm sure you'll agree with me about it.

SOCRATES

What would you do?

STREPSIADES

I'm sure you've seen it at the druggist's stall,
a kind of stone . . . it's beautiful, sparkling, nearly transparent . . .

SOCRATES
> You're referring to the burning glass
> that focuses the sunlight to ignite fires?

STREPSIADES
> Yes. That's it.

SOCRATES
> Go on, tell me your idea.

STREPSIADES
> If I brought it while the lawsuit was being inscribed
> in the court rolls, on the official wax tablets, and held it
> at just the right angle I could melt away the suit in a minute.   840

SOCRATES
> By the Graces, that is ingenious.

STREPSIADES
> It pleases me too,
> having gotten rid of that five-talent lawsuit.

SOCRATES
> Now here's another quibble to practice grabbing quickly.

STREPSIADES
> What is it?

SOCRATES
> Imagine you were on the verge of losing a lawsuit.
> How could you turn it around in your favor the fastest
> if you couldn't call witnesses?

STREPSIADES
> That's simple. I'd do it effortlessly.

SOCRATES

Tell me how.

STREPSIADES

Like this. I'd wait until the trial just before mine was ready
            to start
(though there's small chance of that with the backlog of cases in
            Athens),
and, just as it was about to finish, I'd kill myself.

SOCRATES

That's ridiculous.

STREPSIADES

No, by the gods. They couldn't prosecute me after my death.   850

SOCRATES

That's utter nonsense. Why don't you leave? I won't try to teach
            you any more.

STREPSIADES

Why not? By the gods, please continue, O Socrates.

SOCRATES

But anything you seem to learn you forget almost immediately.
For example, what did I teach you first?

STREPSIADES

Let's see. I know that, but was it first? what was on first?
Wasn't it something about barley flour being kneaded? Was it?

SOCRATES

No. To the crows with him.
He is the most thickheaded forgetful old man I've ever seen.
(Exit Socrates, taking the bedroll with him.)

STREPSIADES

How unlucky I am! Now what will happen to me?
I am ruined. I've failed to learn the art of tongue-twisting
slippery speaking.
O Clouds, I need any advice you can give me.   860

CHORUS

Since you asked us, we'll make a suggestion.
If you have a son of the right age,
send him here to learn in your place.

STREPSIADES

I do have a son, who's just the right type,
but he's refused this education. What should I do?

CHORUS

Has he already inherited your estate?

STREPSIADES

He's big and strong and the pampered son of a very well-
connected mother,
but nonetheless I'll fetch him, no matter what he wishes,
and if he doesn't come along with me, he'll be kicked out of my
house permanently.
If you wait a few minutes I'll bring him over to you.   870
*(Exit Strepsiades. The chorus addresses the Thinkateria and the
Whirlwind cup above its door.)*

CHORUS

Observe that through our power,
you may be granted everything you desire.
See how this old man has been rendered
completely obedient to your wishes,
because you have filled him with awe
and reverence and excitement.

Grasp this opportunity greedily, friend, seize your chance
                       quickly,
for fortune can change things into their opposites almost
                       instantly.
(Enter Strepsiades, kicking and dragging a reluctant Pheidippides.)

STREPSIADES

By the holy Mist, I'm not supporting you another minute.
Take yourself and your extravagant habits to Megacles' mansion,   880
and see if he'll let you gnaw on his marble columns for dinner.

PHEIDIPPIDES

O sacred spirits! Father, what has happened to your brain?
By Olympian Zeus, have you suddenly been struck insane?

STREPSIADES

Look at you, invoking the Olympians. How odd
for a man your age still to consider them gods.

PHEIDIPPIDES

What's odd about that?

STREPSIADES

                       I'm struck by the fashion
in which a boy like you can have such antiquated notions.
Nevertheless, come over here, and soon you'll know better.
I'll teach you something that will make a real man of you,
if you promise not to pass it on to anyone else.   890

PHEIDIPPIDES

Sure. What is it?

STREPSIADES

                       You just swore by Zeus.
Now, you'll see how useful schooling is.
Pheidippides, Zeus does not exist.

PHEIDIPPIDES

What?

STREPSIADES

Whirlwind rules now. Zeus has been overthrown.

PHEIDIPPIDES

I think that's nonsense.

STREPSIADES

Think again. These are the things that *they* believe.

PHEIDIPPIDES

Who agrees with this stuff?

STREPSIADES

Socrates the Melian,
and Chairephon, a man who can track a flea.

PHEIDIPPIDES

You must be out of your mind
to believe lunatics of that kind.   900

STREPSIADES

You need to preserve a reverent silence
and not slander those wise and righteous men.
Besides being clever they're very thrifty.
They don't go out for expensive haircuts
or visit the bathhouses for lascivious massages
with perfumed oils, unlike you, young man,
who've been running through my estate
as if you were already celebrating my wake.
Now hurry up. Come along to learn in my place.

PHEIDIPPIDES

What I am supposed to learn from them?   910

STREPSIADES

    All these things that characterize wise men.
    You'll begin to know yourself, understanding
    that you're both ignorant and dense.
(Strepsiades pauses, thinks for a bit.)
    Wait! I'll be back in a second.
(Strepsiades rushes into his house.)

PHEIDIPPIDES *(sighs)*

    What shall I do? My father has gone insane.
    Should I bring a lawsuit against him
    and have him declared incompetent,
    or should I warn the undertakers
    that he's in the final stage of senile dementia?
(Strepsiades returns, accompanied by a slave carrying two live ducks,
                one male and one female. Throughout the ensuing
                scene the ducks, naturally somewhat uncomfortable
                with the procedure, quack and flap their wings,
                adding to the comic effect.)

STREPSIADES *(pointing to a duck)*

    Look. What do you usually call this? Tell me.   920

PHEIDIPPIDES

    A duck.

STREPSIADES

        And the other one?

PHEIDIPPIDES

                A duck.

STREPSIADES

    Both of them? That's ridiculous.
    In the future, call the male a ducker
    and the female a duckess.

PHEIDIPPIDES

A duckess? Is that a sample of the profound philosophy
you've learned from those . . . motherduckers . . . you've been
            going to see?

STREPSIADES

This, and much more besides. But because I don't have a good
            memory
each thing I had learned I forgot almost immediately.

PHEIDIPPIDES

Did you *forget* your cloak as well?

STREPSIADES

I didn't forget it. I exchanged it for an education.   930

PHEIDIPPIDES

You fool. What happened to your shoes?

STREPSIADES

I dedicated them to higher learning.
Now come on. Move along. Obey your father right away—
even if you consider me mistaken.
I knew you'd be a great orator from the day
you lisped so persuasively
I bought you a toy wagon at the Dasia Festival
with the first obol I earned from jury duty.

PHEIDIPPIDES

Eventually you'll be estranged from these men
and regret that you dragged me over to see them.   940

STREPSIADES

Good. You'll obey.
(*Strepsiades gestures, dismissing the slave with the ducks. The slave
                    enters the house, perhaps first stopping to clean*

up any droppings the ducks have left on the stage.
Strepsiades walks over to the Thinkateria dragging
a reluctant Pheidippides along with him.)

STREPSIADES

                 O Socrates, come here.
Come out here.
(Socrates enters from the Thinkateria door.)
I brought my son. I talked him into coming here.

SOCRATES

He's an intellectual infant. He doesn't know our elevated
            doctrines.

PHEIDIPPIDES

Elevated? I'd like to see you elevated, hangin' by the neck from
            a tree.

STREPSIADES

No! How dare you curse my teacher?

SOCRATES

Notice how he said "hangin'"? How sloppily
he pronounced it, his jaw dropping down so foolishly?
How could he escape major lawsuits or appeal a case persuasively
with his mouth hanging open like a panting dog's in the summer
            heat?   950
Though Hyperbolus did learn it for a talent, and he's not even
            Greek.

STREPSIADES

Don't worry, teacher. He's naturally clever.
When he was a little boy, too young to leave the house,
he made himself a miniature wood boat for a toy,
and he carved himself a chariot, with leather tack,
and even made frogs from pomegranate rinds,

so artistic they nearly seemed alive.
So teach him the arguments, the better, whatever it is,
and the worse, which overturns the better,
and if you can't manage to teach him both of them,   960
at least cover the unjust one, no matter what.

SOCRATES
I won't be here. He shall learn from the Arguments themselves.

STREPSIADES
Just remember, he needs to be able to refute
every kind of lawsuit.
(Exit Socrates. We hear the first line or two of the Better Argument's
speech from off stage, and then he enters.)

BETTER ARGUMENT
Come here. Show yourself
to the spectators. You're certainly unlikely
to be overcome with modesty.
(Enter Worse Argument.)

WORSE ARGUMENT
Lead where you will. Whatever the type of competition,
when we speak to the citizens I always win.

BETTER ARGUMENT
You beat *me*? Who do you think you are?

WORSE ARGUMENT
                                    An Argument.

BETTER ARGUMENT
                            The Worse of the two. 970

WORSE ARGUMENT
Nevertheless, I'll defeat you,
even if they say you're better than me.

BETTER ARGUMENT
    What sort of sneaky tricks will you produce?

WORSE ARGUMENT
                      I'll find some new ideas to use.

BETTER ARGUMENT
    It's only because of their
(pointing to audience)
                foolishness
    you can get away with any of this.

WORSE ARGUMENT
  . Now it's cleverness.

BETTER ARGUMENT
             Nonetheless, it will be vanquished.

WORSE ARGUMENT
    How will you manage it?

BETTER ARGUMENT
               By being the voice of righteousness.

WORSE ARGUMENT
    I'll twist your words around and everything you say I'll
                    contradict.
    I'll claim that Justice doesn't even exist.

BETTER ARGUMENT
                   It doesn't exist?

WORSE ARGUMENT
    If it does, then where is it?

BETTER ARGUMENT
            With the gods.   980

WORSE ARGUMENT

    If Justice is with the gods, then how can it be
    that Zeus imprisoned his father in chains, but himself went free?

BETTER ARGUMENT

    That's sleazy, and what's worse
    is how fashionable this stuff seems to be.
    Someone get me a basin, quick! I think I'm about to be sick.

WORSE ARGUMENT

    You are thirty years out of key with your times.

BETTER ARGUMENT

    And you are a shameless libertine.

WORSE ARGUMENT

                      I resemble that remark.

BETTER ARGUMENT

    A carrion eater who would steal the coins from a dead
           man's eyes.

WORSE ARGUMENT

                    Music to my ears.

BETTER ARGUMENT

    A man who would murder his own father for profit.

WORSE ARGUMENT

    You crown me with gold without knowing it.   990

BETTER ARGUMENT

    Once it would have been known as lead.

WORSE ARGUMENT

    But I consider it an ornament.

BETTER ARGUMENT
Thoroughly brazen.

WORSE ARGUMENT
Typically old-fashioned.

BETTER ARGUMENT
Because of your influence, none of our adolescents
spend their time seeking for genuine knowledge.
But soon all of Athens will know that you're truly ignorant.

WORSE ARGUMENT
And they'll notice you're threadbare and squalid.

BETTER ARGUMENT
And you're undeniably prosperous.
But there was a time when you begged like Telephos,
Euripides' famous character,
a beggar pretending to be a king disguised as a beggar,   1000
exchanging false words for a sack of food.

WORSE ARGUMENT
And wasn't that shrewd?

BETTER ARGUMENT
Absurd.

WORSE ARGUMENT
You'll make me famous.

BETTER ARGUMENT
Handing a son over to you to train
would be a form of child abuse.

WORSE ARGUMENT
And you're too old to be of any use
to this student.

BETTER ARGUMENT
>If I don't save him from your training,
>he'll learn nothing but inane babbling.

WORSE ARGUMENT *(to Pheidippides)*
>Come here. He's not worth your effort.   1010

BETTER ARGUMENT
>If you lay a hand on him, you'll regret it.

CHORUS
>Stop quibbling and bickering with each other,
>but you
(pointing to Better)
>>show the audience how men were taught long ago,
>and you
(pointing to Worse)
>>introduce the new learning to them.
>As you
(pointing to Pheidippides)
>>listen to their learned disputes,
>then choose which school you'll want to attend.

BETTER ARGUMENT
>This is just what I want to do.

WORSE ARGUMENT
>>>Me too.

CHORUS
>Now tell us, which of you will begin?

WORSE ARGUMENT
>I'll yield the first turn to him,
>and I'll take his own words and turn them around   1020
>inventing proverbs and new catch phrases,

using his own arrows to shoot him down
and defeat him. And if he utters
another word, my piercing arguments
will stab his face and his eyes and his mouth
like stinging wasps until he's demolished.

CHORUS
    Now each will rely
    on his cleverness
        and his dexterity,
    his careful language   1030
        and his perspicuity,
    to prove himself the better speaker.
    Of all times, this is the most crucial
    to determine wisdom's future.
    Gather round closely, my friends,
    this is a very important contest.

    Now you, who taught our ancient forebears the things which
                made them great,
    raise your proud voice in praise of your own nature.

BETTER ARGUMENT
    I will tell you how our culture was taught long ago,
    when justice and moderation and I all flourished.   1040
    The voices of shouting children never were heard.
    They walked in an orderly fashion down the road
    to their music lessons, and never complained,
    even when the snow poured down in gigantic flakes.
    In their music classes they practiced and memorized gladly,
    not distracting themselves by rubbing their thighs together.
    They sang of "Magnificent Pallas, Destroyer of Cities"
    and "Blow bugle blow, the horns boldly crying,"
    following the traditional arrangements.
    And if any of the boys tried to modify the songs   1050
    by substituting suggestive lyrics or adding intricate harmonies

or musical flourishes in the style of Phrynis,
he would be beaten and abused as an enemy of the Muses.
In the gymnasium, while sitting naked, the boys were required
to cross their legs modestly, and not expose themselves
                    indecently.
And they'd sweep and smooth the sand when they stood up,
not tempting lascivious spectators with images of their buttocks.
The boys were taught not to rub liniment below their navels,
causing foam to flow shamefully over their downy triangles,
nor lisp effeminately to their lovers, nor stroll along   1060
casting sidelong glances at passing men
as though they were acting as their own pimps.
And when they were dining they'd be taught
not to gobble up the most expensive dishes,
nor shake their heads and snatch the elaborate garnishes
away from their elders, nor giggle, nor cross their legs
                    suggestively.

WORSE ARGUMENT
    He's one of those old fashioned men who wear
    gold cicadas in their hair to prove how long their families have
                    lived here,
    and attend the equally antiquated Ox-Killing Festivals.

BETTER ARGUMENT
    These were the teachings that won the Battle of Marathon for us. 1070
    You bring up children who shiver in thick cloaks at the slightest
                    of breezes,
    and when dancing at the Panathenaic festival behave
                    outrageously,
    being so weak that their shields droop nearly down to their
                    knees,
    dishonoring the great warrior goddess Athena.
    For these reasons, young man, you should choose the Better
                    Argument confidently.
    You should disdain the bathhouses and distrust the law courts
                    and marketplace,

and when your elders approach, rise up from your seat, and not
        misbehave

toward your parents, nor do the shameful things that disgrace the
        very names

of Modesty and Shame. You shouldn't dart into the houses of
        dancing girls,

or flirt with whores on the street, destroying your reputation for
        chastity,   1080

nor contradict your elderly father, referring to him as an "old
        fart,"

nor remind him of the infirmities of age, acquired over the years
        he spent raising you.

WORSE ARGUMENT

By Dionysus, if you are persuaded by him, young man,

you'll be compared to Hippocrates' sons. Everyone will say you're
        such a fool

that, though grown up, you still live on baby food.

BETTER ARGUMENT

You would spend your time in the wrestling schools,

and your skin would be healthy and tanned and smooth,

not like today's youth, who hang out in the marketplace telling
        crude jokes.

Nor would you be dragged into sleazy disputations and vicious
        legal actions,

but you'd go into the groves of the sacred olives, practicing your
        running,   1090

with well-behaved friends, and win the prizes at athletic contests,

being crowned with white reeds, under the lovely and fragrant
        yew trees.

You'd watch the wind rippling the leaves, revealing their silver
        undersides,

delighting in the season's sounds and sights,

and the rustling of the breeze through the elms and planes.

(The following section is a pnigos, *a speech normally recited very quickly,*
        ideally all on a single breath.)

If you follow my lead and do as I say
and practice the things that I recommend,
your chest will always glisten with healthy sweat,
your arms will be strong and your shoulders broad,
you'll have narrow lips and muscular hips,   1100
and a very impressive penis.
But if you choose what most men now do,
you'll have a narrow chest and no biceps,
you'll have flabby skin,
and your legs will be thin,
and your mouth and your briefs both will be big
with decrees and proposals for the assembly.
He'll convince you to consider evil things worthwhile,
and to think good deeds are utterly vile,
and after a while you'll notice   1110
you've become like Antimachus,
with an indelible brown stain on your nose.

CHORUS

What a beautiful tower of labor and learning,
your words have conjured before us.
They remind us of a happier time
when men lived wisely and chastely.
Now against this you,
(pointing to Worse Argument)
with your effete Muse,
will need to speak of your new innovations.
Since the Better Argument is well respected,
you'll need powerful rhetoric to defeat him.   1120
Unless you do, everyone will laugh at you.

WORSE ARGUMENT

I've been waiting eagerly for my chance
to annihilate his claims with their opposites.
Although I am known as the Worse Argument,
the smartest men know me as the first

to reexamine the established notions of ethics and justice
in order to contradict them. Even supporting the worse cause,
I've always won, something worthy of immense amounts of
      money.
If we look closer at his type of education,
I'll refute him and win you over.   1130
First he tried to dissuade you from taking warm baths.
What was the reason for that?

BETTER ARGUMENT

They're such an effeminate habit; they'll turn men into cowards.

WORSE ARGUMENT

Wait. I've just caught you by the waist in an unbreakable hold.
You won't be able to escape. Now, tell me:
of all the gods' mortal children, which do you consider the
      bravest?
Who was best at toiling the hardest and laboring the longest?

BETTER ARGUMENT

I would say that Heracles was clearly the best.

WORSE ARGUMENT

And aren't the most famous hot springs called the baths of
      Heracles?
Yet you called him the bravest.   1140

BETTER ARGUMENT

These things . . . these are the sorts of ones
young men are babbling about all day long,
so they fill the baths and empty the wrestling grounds.

WORSE ARGUMENT

Next, you complained about men hanging around the
      marketplace.
I, on the other hand, would like to praise the courts and markets.

If they were wicked, Homer never would have sung
that Nestor and all the other wise men were constantly speaking
      in them.
From here, I'll return to young men exercising their tongues.
He's says it's not necessary for them to practice with it, but I say
      it is.
He also recommends chastity. But I say he's wrong about both of
      these.   1150
Whenever did anyone gain anything good by being chaste?
Can you say anything to contradict this?

BETTER ARGUMENT

                          Of course.
Because of his chastity, Peleus was given a sword.

WORSE ARGUMENT

A sword? And what a wonderful bit of luck that was.
Hyperbolus the Lampmaker earned thousands of talents
through his dishonest use of words, but never, by Zeus, a sword.

BETTER ARGUMENT

And on account of his chastity, Peleus was allowed to marry
      Thetis.

WORSE ARGUMENT

See? And then she left him. Because of his lack of experience,
he couldn't please her in the bedclothes. Women don't want that
      sort of innocence,
They like far more sophisticated sex. See what a useless old relic
      you are!   1160
Look, young man, at what his version of self-control lacks.
If you follow his path, see how many pleasures you'll need to
      forsake:
girls and boys and gourmet food, drinking contests and good
      booze,

loud music with suggestive lyrics, rowdy shouting and
        extravagant spending,
all the things that make life worth living. Do you wish to give
        these up for him?
But what if you decide you wish to do it? Can you escape the laws
        of nature?
What if your instincts overtake you, and you make some mistake,
perhaps commit adultery and are caught and convicted?
You'll be unable to speak in your own favor.
But if you associate with me, you can let loose freely,   1170
indulging your nature and thinking nothing shameful.
And if you're caught with some man's wife, you can argue
        successfully.
You can say you did nothing wrong. You can bring in Zeus as
        evidence.
If he, king of the gods, is a slave to love and women,
how can anyone expect you, a mere mortal, to be stronger than
        him in resisting them?

BETTER ARGUMENT

But what if he follows your advice and gets convicted?
He'll be condemned to the adulterer's punishment,
the public humiliation of having his pubic hair plucked out,
his genitals seared with burning ashes, and a turnip pounded up
        his anus?
Does he have some clever maxim to save you from a distended
        asshole?   1180

WORSE ARGUMENT

And what's wrong with having a slightly wider ass?

BETTER ARGUMENT

                  What could be worse than that?

WORSE ARGUMENT

What will you do if I defeat you on this point?

BETTER ARGUMENT
   I'll be silent. What else could I manage?

WORSE ARGUMENT
                                    Now, tell me.
   How do you usually refer to lawyers?

BETTER ARGUMENT
                              As assholes.

WORSE ARGUMENT
                                    So do I.
   Now what about actors?

BETTER ARGUMENT
                        Even bigger assholes.

WORSE ARGUMENT
                                 Precisely.
   And politicians?

BETTER ARGUMENT
             The biggest assholes of them all.

WORSE ARGUMENT
                                       Then
   you know you've been talking nonsense all along.
   Now, examine the audience. Who are in the majority?

BETTER ARGUMENT
   Even I can see that.

WORSE ARGUMENT
             What, precisely, do you see?

BETTER ARGUMENT
    Lots of them, by the gods.   1190
    Hundreds of assholes. That one, over there,
    and definitely that one, and him, too,
    and especially the one with the long hair.

WORSE ARGUMENT
    So now, what do you say?

BETTER ARGUMENT
    I've been defeated. Here, you assholes,
    take my cloak, I'm deserting to your side.
    (Better takes off his cloak and tosses it off stage ahead of him as he exits.
                    Strepsiades enters.)

WORSE ARGUMENT
    What next? Do you want to take your son back,
    or should I teach him how to speak?

STREPSIADES
    Teach him and, if you need to, beat him too.
    Remember to train him well for me in the Other Argument,   1200
    so out of one side of his mouth he can handle minor lawsuits
    while the other side is trained for the major cases.

WORSE ARGUMENT
    Don't worry. I'll make him a clever sophist.

PHEIDIPPIDES *(aside)*
    What I'd call a sallow, pathetic son-of-a-bitch.
    (Exit Pheidippides and Worse Argument into the Thinkateria;
                    Strepsiades goes back into his own house.)

CHORUS
    Goodbye. I think that soon you'll regret this.
    Now we want to tell the judges how they'll profit, if they treat
                    us well,

and award us first prize in this dancing contest, as would only
            be just.
If you can be persuaded to vote in favor of us,
when it's the season to sow new crops in your fields,
we'll send the rain to you first, and to others later.   1210
Then, when your land produces corn and grapes,
we'll protect them until the harvest,
not drying them out or drowning them.
But if any mortal forgets to honor us as goddesses,
he should be aware of the evils with which we will curse him.
From his lands, he'll never receive wine, nor any other crops.
If the olives or grape vines ripen,
we'll knock them down with our icy arrows.
And if we see him making sun-baked bricks, we'll rain,
and bombard his roof tiles with our heaviest hail.   1220
And if he or his family or friends are having a marriage
            procession,
we'll rain so hard the entire night, that he might even wish
he were living in Egypt, instead of having judged us unfairly.
*(Enter Strepsiades, counting dejectedly. He is carrying a bundle, which
            will at line 1242 be revealed as a cloak.)*
Five, four, three, and then two,
and after that the day I hate worst of all,
the day I fear and tremble and feel ill,
because after it comes the Old and New Day,
when the moon is both old and new,
and all my payments are due.
Each of my creditors has sworn that he'll give a deposit to the
            court   1230
arranging to prosecute a lawsuit against me.
They swear they will crush me and squeeze me dry,
and when I reply with a fair and reasonable request:
"Dear Sir, please don't do this just yet,"
or "Delay some of it," or "Discharge the debt,"
they never relent. Instead, they treat me like a thief,
and then abuse me and threaten to sue me for everything they
            can get.

Now let them sue. And see how little they profit by it,
if Pheidippides has learned the art of speaking well.
I'll know in an instant. I'll knock on the door of the Thinkateria
        here.   1240
   Boy! Come here! Boy? Boy!
(Socrates opens doors and enters.)

SOCRATES
                    I greet you, O Strepsiades.

STREPSIADES
   And I, you. First take this.
(Strepsiades opens the bundle in his arms, revealing a good wool cloak.
              Socrates takes it and tosses it inside to a waiting
              slave or student.)
   A man should honor his teacher appropriately.
   Now, tell me about my son. Has he learned the Argument
   that you introduced us to?

SOCRATES
   He has learned it.

STREPSIADES
               O Fraud, you marvelous Empress!

SOCRATES
   Now you shall escape your lawsuits as you wish.

STREPSIADES
   Even if they prove I borrowed the money by using witnesses?

SOCRATES
   Even if thousands of them appear in their defense.
   The more the better.   1250

STREPSIADES
   Now I'll shout loudly to all the moneylenders
   that it's their turn to weep and worry.

They won't get the principal back,
nor the interest, nor the interest on the interest,
and they'll never pester me again.
For you've reared a son for me in here,
with a two-edged sword for a tongue.
who will be like a breakwater before my house,
protecting my person and property
from the enemies trying to harm me.   1260
He shall free his old father from all his troubles.
Now, go running inside and call him for me.
O child, O son, come out of there,
if you can hear the voice of your father.
(Enter Socrates and Pheidippides. Pheidippides is now dressed like one of
the Thinkateriasts, his cloak and shoes gone and his
robe a bit worse for the wear.)

SOCRATES
    Here's your man.

STREPSIADES
    My dear, dear son.

SOCRATES
    Take him away.
(Exit Socrates.)

STREPSIADES
    Oh, oh! My child!
                    Ah, ah!
    I am overjoyed to see you looking so pale and unhealthy.
    Now anyone who meets you will recognize your abilities   1270
    in disputes, denials, and refutations, and all the skills for which
                    our city is famous.
    A false innocence blooms on your cheeks, asking, "What does
                    that mean?"
    and making you look like the injured party although you've done
                    the injury,

even if caught flagrantly in the act. Anyone can see that
your face is typically Attic. You'll save me now,
just as you ruined me earlier.

PHEIDIPPIDES
  What do you fear?

STREPSIADES
                    The Old and New Day.

PHEIDIPPIDES
  How can there be one day which is both new and old?

STREPSIADES
  It's the one on which they deposit the court fees.

PHEIDIPPIDES
  Then they'll lose their deposits. It's impossible   1280
  for a single day to become two days.

STREPSIADES
                    Why?

PHEIDIPPIDES
  Why? For precisely the same reason
  that the same woman can't become
  both an old and a young one.

STREPSIADES
                    But that's what the laws say. Isn't it customary?

PHEIDIPPIDES
  I don't think they interpreted the law correctly.

STREPSIADES
                    Aren't there precedents?

PHEIDIPPIDES
  Solon, the ancient lawmaker, was a lover of the people at heart.

STREPSIADES
> What has that to do with the Old and the New?

PHEIDIPPIDES
> As I was saying: he created two separate days
> for this procedure, the Old and the New.
> The deposits were to be made at the New Moon.   1290

STREPSIADES
> Then why was the Old added to it?

PHEIDIPPIDES
>   For this reason, my good man:
> so the accused could come forward one day in advance
> and try to settle out of court. If this didn't work,
> the litigants would meet the next morning at dawn.

STREPSIADES
> Then why don't the judges accept the deposits on the
>   New Moon,
> rather than on the Old and New?

PHEIDIPPIDES
> I think they're like professional wine tasters,
> wanting to sample the deposits as soon as they're made,
> and taking small samples away rather than waiting a day.

STREPSIADES
> Well said, indeed. Why do you unfortunate fools   1300
(pointing at audience)
> just sit there like stones, dupes of the cunning and the wise,
> like a bunch of sheep ready for fleecing,
> crowded together in a messy heap?
> Now I need to sing an exalted song
> praising our newfound prosperity.

O blessed Strepsiades, how wise you were,
such a clever son to rear.
All my friends and my neighbors
will say admiringly
when speaking eloquently,   1310
you win your lawsuits.
Now let's go inside so I can feast you.
(Pheidippides and Strepsiades go into their house. A few seconds later the
First Creditor and his witness enter.)

FIRST CREDITOR *(to witness, as if continuing an earlier conversation)*
    . . . and that a man should be deprived of his own property.
    No, never! It would have been better to have said no
                            immediately,
    no matter how embarrassing it is to refuse a favor to a neighbor,
    than to be placed in this situation.
    So now, for the sake of my own money, I'm forced
    to drag you over here as a witness
    and endure the hatred of a neighbor.
    But as long as I live, I'll never let down my native land,   1320
    and her reputation for litigation, so:
(raising voice in official manner)
    "I officially summon Strepsiades . . ."
(Strepsiades, who has been listening from his doorway for a few lines,
                        steps forward.)

STREPSIADES
                                What do you want?

FIRST CREDITOR
    For you to appear on the Old and New Day.

STREPSIADES *(to witness)*
                                    Witness for me
    that he said on two days. About what?

FIRST CREDITOR
> The twelve minas of mine you borrowed
> to buy the dark horse.

STREPSIADES
> Horse? Did you notice what he just said?
> Everyone knows I hate horses.

FIRST CREDITOR
> And by Zeus, you swore by the gods you'd pay me back.

STREPSIADES
> Not now, by Zeus, for my son Pheidippides has mastered
> the Irrefutable Argument.   1330

FIRST CREDITOR
> And because of that, you intend to refuse to pay back your debt?

STREPSIADES
> What other advantage would I get from his having learned it?

FIRST CREDITOR
> And will you swear by the gods to what you just said,
> in whatever holy place I ask you to repeat it?

STREPSIADES
> What sort of gods?

FIRST CREDITOR
> Zeus and Hermes and Poseidon.

STREPSIADES
> By Zeus,
> just for the pleasure of swearing at them, I'll add in another three
> obols.

FIRST CREDITOR
    If you continue in these blasphemous ways,
    you'll come to a bad end one of these days.
    *(Strepsiades reaches over casually and pats the first creditor's rather
                    substantial paunch.)*

STREPSIADES
    This hide of yours could use a good tanning.

FIRST CREDITOR
    Ugh! You're making fun of me.

STREPSIADES
                    I think it would do for a gallon or two. 1340

FIRST CREDITOR
    By Zeus the Great and the other gods, you will not escape
    punishment for your effrontery.

STREPSIADES
                    Wonderful. I'm delighted by these gods of yours;
    for us men of education, swearing by Zeus is one of the funniest
                    things we've heard.

FIRST CREDITOR
    Eventually the gods will punish you. But for now,
    just return my money and I'll leave in a hurry.

STREPSIADES
                                    Wait. Stay there.
    In a second I'll answer you clearly.
    (Exit Strepsiades into his house.)

FIRST CREDITOR *(to witness)*
    What is it likely that he'll do?

WITNESS
　　It would be reasonable for him to repay you.
　　(Enter Strepsiades, followed by a slave carrying the female duck.)

STREPSIADES
　　Where is that ignorant creditor of mine? Now, tell me what you
　　　　　　call this.

FIRST CREDITOR
　　What do I call it? A duck.   1350

STREPSIADES
　　I'd never give an obol to a man so ignorant
　　he can't tell a duckess from a hole in the ground.

FIRST CREDITOR
　　You won't repay the money you owe?

STREPSIADES
　　　　　　　　　　　　　　　　　I don't think so.
　　Now, if you're finished with me, would you mind not blocking
　　　　　　my door?
　　Now, go!

FIRST CREDITOR
　　　　　　I'm going. But I want you to know
　　that I'm making my deposit early tomorrow morning.

STREPSIADES
　　Then you will throw it away along with your twelve minas.
　　Don't do it. You don't deserve to lose this too, just because
　　in your well-intentioned ignorance you called my duckess
　　　　　　a duck.
*(Exit first creditor and witness. Strepsiades gestures to the slave, who goes
　　　　　　into Strepsiades' house with the duck, perhaps first
　　　　　　cleaning up anything the duck has left on the stage.*

Just as Strepsiades is about to follow him through
the door, the Second Creditor enters, sobbing
and wailing. His expensive clothing is torn and
spattered with mud, and his face and hands are
streaked with blood.)

SECOND CREDITOR
Alas! Oh me! O poor me!   1360

STREPSIADES *(looking around)*
                    Oh?
What could be the source of such wailing cries? Did one of the
                    demons
from Carcinnus' melodramas utter that noise?

SECOND CREDITOR *(still wiping blood away from his eyes)*
Who wishes to know what sort of thing I am?
I'm a very unfortunate man.

STREPSIADES
Can you keep your misfortunes to yourself?

SECOND CREDITOR
Oh, how cruel the gods and how harsh my fate!
To have the wheel of my chariot break!
O poor Tlempolemus, suffering the vengeance of the gods!

STREPSIADES
What has the fate of Tlempolemus to do with yours?
*(Second creditor finally finishes cleaning himself up and wiping his eyes
and recognizes Strepsiades.)*

SECOND CREDITOR
Stop making fun of me and tell your son to repay me the money 1370
I loaned to him. Fortune has not been good to me.

STREPSIADES

What is this money you're asking for?

SECOND CREDITOR

The money that he borrowed.

STREPSIADES

It seems to me that you have some genuine problems.

SECOND CREDITOR

By the gods, I would agree with that. I just fell out of my chariot.

STREPSIADES

Are you talking nonsense because you landed on your ass?

SECOND CREDITOR

What's nonsensical about wanting to recover the money I lent?

STREPSIADES

You obviously haven't recovered your wits from the crash.

SECOND CREDITOR

What?

STREPSIADES

It appears your brains were shaken up
when you crashed and landed on your butt.

SECOND CREDITOR

By Hermes, I'm going to summon you to court immediately   1380
if you don't pay back the silver you owe me.

STREPSIADES

First, tell me what you think:
does Zeus send down new water each time it rains,
or does the sun draw up and drop down the same water again?

SECOND CREDITOR
> I don't know or care about such such things.

STREPSIADES
> How can you justly recover your silver
> if you don't understand heavenly matters?

SECOND CREDITOR
> If you can't pay back the entire amount,
> just give me the interest now.

STREPSIADES
> What makes it so interesting?   1390

SECOND CREDITOR
> It grows larger and larger by the month and the day,
> making your money all flow away.

STREPSIADES
>   Definitely clever.
> But then, would you consider the ocean to be larger today than
>   yesterday?

SECOND CREDITOR
> No, by God, the same. For it to be larger would violate
> the laws of nature.

STREPSIADES
>   What a greedy fool you are!
> If it's unnatural for the sea to grow larger from the influx of the
>   rivers,
> then why should more silver flow in to enlarge your wallet?
> Now take yourself off, away from my house.
> *(Strepsiades pauses, waiting for the second creditor to leave. After a few*
> *seconds, he calls into the house to a slave.)*
>   Boy! Bring me a whip!

SECOND CREDITOR *(to chorus and audience)*
You're witnesses to this.

STREPSIADES *(flourishing whip)*
Now trot away. Why are you waiting?   1400
Why don't you ride off, you old lame horse?
(strikes second creditor)

SECOND CREDITOR
Wouldn't this clearly be a case of aggravated assault?

STREPSIADES
                                        Hurry, or we'll see
if you'd gallop any faster with this whip shoved up your
                    thoroughbred asshole.
*(Exit second creditor, with Strepsiades cracking the whip menacingly
                    behind him.)*
You're fleeing? I'd meant that to speed you along
with your pairs of horses and chariot wheels.
(Exit Strepsiades into his house.)

CHORUS
How easy it is to be seized by a love for evil!
Everything this old man desires now
is completely unethical.
He wants to evade his debts dishonestly.
He wasn't like this until recently,   1410
and soon he'll forsake these sophistries,
learning how vile they really can be.
I think that soon he will discover
that, just as much as he once
wished his son to undermine justice
        and win debates
against everyone he might meet,
        through his depravity,

now, just as much he'll wish his son
    were voiceless.   1420
(Enter Strepsiades, pursued and whipped by Pheidippides with the very
                    same whip with which Strepsiades attacked the
                    second creditor. The flogging continues through line
                    1434, and then as necessary.)

STREPSIADES
    Ow! Ow!
    O friends, relatives, and countrymen,
    help me avenge this outrage.
    He's beat me in every way you can imagine!
    My head and my cheeks! You brutal bastard!
    You're beating your *father*!

PHEIDIPPIDES
                    Yes, father, I am.

STREPSIADES
    See! He admits that he's beating me!

PHEIDIPPIDES
                      I am, indeed.

STREPSIADES
    You murderous vandal and blasphemous scoundrel!

PHEIDIPPIDES
    Go on and call me a few more names.
    You know how I enjoy being called such things.   1430

STREPSIADES
    The world's biggest asshole.

PHEIDIPPIDES
    It's like being pelted with rose petals.
    (strikes Strepsiades again)

STREPSIADES
>You're striking your father!

PHEIDIPPIDES
>   By God, I'll show you,
>how right I was when I struck you.

STREPSIADES
>   You godforsaken creature!
>How can it be right to strike your father?

STREPSIADES
>I can prove it. In a sense,
>it will be a victory in a speaking contest.

STREPSIADES
>How can you win?

PHEIDIPPIDES
>   Easily. And by a significant margin.
>Choose which of the two Arguments you wish to support.

STREPSIADES
>Which arguments?

PHEIDIPPIDES
>   The Better or the Worse.   1440

STREPSIADES
>By Zeus, I have had you taught well, my good friend,
>to contradict every type of Justice, if you intend
>to convince me it's good and just
>for fathers to be beaten by their sons.

PHEIDIPPIDES
>If you listen, I think I'll convince you,
>in a way you cannot refute.

STREPSIADES

> I'd like to hear what you have to say for yourself.

CHORUS

> Your task, old man, will not be easy.
> To overpower him, you'll need to think quickly.
> He is likely to be quite persuasive,   1450
> because he is confident, and free to be insolent,
> and he'll do anything to win.
> But first, tell us just how your fight began.
> Tell us everything that happened then.

STREPSIADES

> I'll tell you about the very beginning of our quarrel.
> as you know, we were feasting. So, of course,
> I asked him to take the lyre and sing Simonides' song,
> the one called "How the Lamb Was Shorn."
> And the first thing he said was that harp-playing was old-
>   fashioned,
> and when gentlemen drink, they shouldn't sing like women
>   hulling wheat.   1460

PHEIDIPPIDES

> And shouldn't he have been beaten for that immediately?
> Asking me to sing for my supper as if I were one of those cicadas
> Athenians would wear in Solon's grandfather's day,
> to show their native ancestry.

STREPSIADES

> These things he's saying now are just the kind he said inside.
> He even claimed that Simonides was an overrated poet.
> I could hardly restrain myself, but I held back at first.
> I asked him to take the traditional myrtle branch,
> and perhaps recite some Aeschylus to me instead, but then
>   he said:
> "I, too, consider Aeschylus the best of the poets   1470

for empty noise and ranting, and incoherence and bombast."
At that point, I could feel my heart shaking with rage,
but again, I bit back my anger and said:
"Why don't you recite some stuff by the more modern guys—
whichever of their clever things you like."
And then, he launched into some scene by Euripides
in which a brother is seducing his sister by the same mother!
I couldn't restrain myself any longer, but stood up and
        interrupted
all the disgusting things he'd been saying, and as you'd expect,
we started to shout, getting louder and louder. And then up he
        leaped,   1480
and started to pulverize and pound and choke and beat me.

PHEIDIPPIDES

    And wasn't I right? He refused to see the beauty of Euripides!

STREPSIADES

    That filth! Beautiful? What should I call you? You . . .
    But I'd just be beaten again.

PHEIDIPPIDES

                And rightly, by Zeus.

STREPSIADES

    You blasphemous ingrate! To say that to the father who raised
        you up.
    When I heard you lisping as a baby, I learned to understand you
        completely.
    When you said "dwing" I knew you wanted a drink,
    but if you went "oo" I went to bring you some food,
    and if you barely started to say "kakka,"
    I took you outdoors and held you up.   1490
    And when you were throttling me now,
    so I was crying and screaming
        and nearly crapping my shorts,

you wouldn't even help me
    outdoors, you creep,
but instead, you continued to choke the crap out of me.

CHORUS
    I suppose the hearts of the young
        will leap with joy
    when Pheidippides speaks.
        If after the things he's done today,   1500
    persuasive words
        can keep him safe,
    the skin of old men
        will be worth less
    than a bunch
        of watercress.

PHEIDIPPIDES
    The newest modes of speech and thought are wonderful.
    I have no trouble now despising established laws and customs.
    Once, the only things I knew were horses,
    and I couldn't put three words together   1510
    without committing some sort of solecism,
    but then he made me stop my horseplay,
    and go acquire wisdom,
    scrutinize complex thoughts and subtle meanings.
    Now I think I can teach him how it's right for me
    to chastise and beat him.

STREPSIADES
    By Zeus, could you go back to your horses? It would be easier
    for me to support a *four*-horse chariot than to be beaten.

PHEIDIPPIDES
    Now, returning to the point where you interrupted,
    I'll begin by asking: When I was a child, did you beat me?   1520

STREPSIADES

Of course I did, with the best intentions. I was a caring parent.

PHEIDIPPIDES

Then isn't it right that I should intend the best toward you?
And if intending the best is synonymous with beating,
then how could it be that I should be struck and your body
            should go unpunished?
Obviously, if you're a free man, then so am I.
You think it "right that the children should weep and the father
            shouldn't"?
You feel that beating is appropriate only to children?
I reply that old men are in their second childhood,
and it's even more reasonable for the old than the young to weep,
because at their age it's less natural to make mistakes.   1530

STREPSIADES

I've never heard of a place where it's customary for fathers to
            suffer like this.

PHEIDIPPIDES

These laws and traditions were invented by men like you and me,
who by their skill in speaking, had decrees passed in the
            Assembly.
So isn't it possible for me now to make a law that henceforward
sons should return the blows they've received from their fathers?
Now, for the blows we'd suffered, before this law was enacted,
we'll freely grant amnesty. Consider the birds and other beasts:
they all fight with their fathers. And what are the differences
            between us and them,
except that they don't write legislation?

STREPSIADES

If you want to live just like a bird,   1540
why don't you eat excrement and sleep on a perch?

PHEIDIPPIDES

    My good man, that is not the same thing, at least
    it does not seem so to Socrates.

STREPSIADES

                    In that case, don't beat me,
    or else you'll have no one to blame but yourself.

PHEIDIPPIDES

    What do you mean?

STREPSIADES

                If it's right for you to punish me,
    then what will happen when your son is born?

PHEIDIPPIDES

                   But I might not have one.
    and then I would have been beaten in vain, and you would have
            died mocking me.

STREPSIADES

    Old men, I'm sorry to say, he's speaking very logically.
    I think I'm forced to agree that it's just and equitable
    for us to be beaten if we don't behave righteously.   1550

PHEIDIPPIDES

    Let's examine another convention.

STREPSIADES

                   It will be the death of me.

PHEIDIPPIDES

    It will help you feel better about the beatings you've suffered.

STREPSIADES

    What? Do you intend to teach me how beatings are good for me?

PHEIDIPPIDES
>No. I intend to beat my mother just as I beat you.

STREPSIADES
>   What? What are you saying?
>This is even worse than all the rest.

PHEIDIPPIDES
>I can win another victory with this new idea.
>My argument will prove that it's both necessary and proper
>to beat my mother.

STREPSIADES
>   What will you say next?
>You'll end up being thrown into an unmarked grave
>with the paupers and criminals and Socrates,   1560
>and that Worse Argument of his.
>*(to the Clouds)*
>O Clouds, it was because of you I yearned
>for these vile things. You are the cause of all of this.

CHORUS
>No, you are the source of all your own trouble.
>You turned voluntarily to these foul practices.

STREPSIADES
>Why didn't you warn me about this earlier
>instead of tempting an innocent old man into error?

CHORUS
>This is how we treat everybody.
>If we know you have evil tendencies
>we tempt you to do unethical deeds,   1570

until the wrong you do rebounds on you
and you learn to respect and dread the gods.

STREPSIADES

O Clouds, I did deserve my misfortunes.
It wasn't necessary for me to withhold the money I owed
fraudulently. Now, my dearest son,
let's go see Socrates and that disgusting Chairephon.
I'll ruin them along with me. Let's assault them.

PHEIDIPPIDES

I could not treat my teachers so badly.

STREPSIADES

Of course, you should worship the Paternal Zeus.

PHEIDIPPIDES

Listen to that. Paternal Zeus? How absurdly old-fashioned.   1580
Zeus doesn't even exist.

STREPSIADES

He does.

PHEIDIPPIDES

No, Zeus doesn't.
Whirlwind is now the king, having overthrown him.

STREPSIADES

No, he wasn't overthrown, but I was mistakenly convinced
by that pot over there, painted to resemble a Whirlwind.
I even persuaded you to take a cheap piece of clay for a god.

PHEIDIPPIDES

You've gone insane and started raving.
(*Exit Pheidippides back into the Thinkateria.*)

STREPSIADES

    I must have gone mad. Only insanity could have made me
    reject the gods on account of Socrates.
(turning to Herm)
    O friend Hermes, don't be angry or seek to destroy me,
    but forgive me instead for my foolishness   1590
    and my momentary insanity, and give me advice.
    Should I prosecute them with a lawsuit?
(Strepsiades pauses, listening for an answer from Herm.)
    He says not. He exhorts me to avoid the law courts.
    Instead, he said, I should go quickly and set the house
    of those madmen on fire.
(to slave off stage)
                             Come here, Xanthias, come here,
    bringing a ladder and pitchfork.
    Climb up to the top of the Thinkateria
    and bring down the roof, if you love your master.
(This scene should be one of massive and nearly festive confusion. Ideally,
                   several slaves [or stagehands] should be running
                   around with ladders and axes and pitchforks,
                   dismantling the Thinkateria backdrop, prying up
                   and throwing down wood planks, yelling, enjoying
                   the activity of arson and the opportunities for
                   larceny, and perhaps indulging in a few steps from
                   a cordax dance. The chorus could help out.)
    Cast down their house about them.
(to another slave)
    Bring me a torch, blazing brightly,   1600
    and I'll set the night on fire,
    like a torchlight parade.
    I'll exact my own justice on those quacks
    for the harm that they have done to me.
(Students appear and disappear as shadowy figures lean out of the
                 partially dismantled walls of the Thinkateria.
                 Slaves have piled firewood around the exits so that

the Thinkateriasts cannot leave the burning
building.)

STUDENT 1
Ow! Ow!

STREPSIADES *(to slave)*
Take another torch and start more flames.

STUDENT 1
What are you doing?

STREPSIADES *(taking an axe to the pillar supporting the*
Whirlwind cup)
Demolishing the support for your Arguments.

STUDENT 1
Who is burning down our home?

STREPSIADES
The man whose cloak you stole.

STUDENT 1
You'll kill us. You're killing us!
(Strepsiades climbs up a ladder and begins chopping at the rafters.)

STREPSIADES
That's precisely what I'm trying to accomplish,
as long as my pitchfork does its work and I don't fall off the
ladder   1610
breaking my neck.
(Socrates appears through a hole in the wall.)

SOCRATES
What are you doing there on the roof?

STREPSIADES
> I'm walking on air and contemplating the flames from a
> > second sun.

SOCRATES
> You worthless idiot.
> *(coughing and gasping)*
> > > I'm going to suffocate.

STREPSIADES
> Now you've earned your due for the outrages
> you've done to the gods, and prying into the secrets of the moon.
> *(to slaves and chorus)*
> > Hunt them down and shower them with blows
> > for all the wrongs they have done to the gods.
> *(Exit Strepsiades. Slaves throw paving stones and wood at the students.*
> > > *The conflagration turns into a riotous celebration.*
> > > *The chorus accompanies the general destruction*
> > > *with singing and dancing. After a few minutes, the*
> > > *slaves exit, and as the lights dim on the embers of*
> > > *the Thinkateria the chorus marches out.)*

CHORUS *(softly, and perhaps sadly)*
> Let us go away. We have danced our part for the day.

Birds

Translated by
Paul Muldoon with Richard Martin

Translator's Preface

Richard Martin

Why *birds*? Maybe this is the wrong question to ask of Aristophanes. After all, his goal as a comic poet competing in the Athenian dramatic contests was the same as any stand-up artist's: make people laugh. If it meant putting on a chorus who floated like clouds, wore stings like wasps, or croaked like frogs, he did it (in 423, 422, and 405 B.C. respectively). Maybe birds were not quite funny enough. When his play named for them was produced in late March 414 at the festival of the City Dionysia, it placed second. First prize went to the *Party-goers* (*Komastai*) by Ameipsias, of which not a trace survived but which no doubt had a raucous, good-time chorus. Even live bird action and costuming to rival Vegas could not have trumped the staging of a drunken free-for-all that evoked the very origin of the dramatic form; for comedy's etymology—"singing at the *komos*"—acknowledges its roots in the informal, post-party performances (*komoi*) of unrestrained revelers out to insult the world. Bringing that kind of frenzy into the Theater of Dionysus was probably, for Ameipsias, a sure-fire way to win, like a pie fight in later avatars of the genre. Aristophanes' *Birds* is far more intellectual.

This intellectuality has been an interpretive problem ever since. Unlike the earlier plays among the eleven that survive, *Birds* does not lampoon, lambaste, degrade, disfigure, and detract—at least, not very much. Of course, there are easy scores made of dithyrambic poets and informers, quack scientist types and religious frauds. But these are minor episodes, fodder for pratfalls, dramatic equivalents of the one-liner. There are no sustained, relentless attacks on well-known demagogues, no denunciations of the stupid war that had embroiled Athens and Sparta since Aristophanes first began his career. It is difficult to put the play in a context, even though we know the date of its production. Is it a warning about the limits of Athenian imperialism? A dreamlike fantasy about building Utopia? A beaker parody of a fantasy? What are its targets: sophistry and rhetoric, Athenian meddlesomeness, impiety, or acquisitive human nature? Or is the comedy something new on the scene, a noninvasive procedure, a philosophical "what if," play-as-thought-experiment?

These positions and more have been argued since the early nineteenth century. Like its chorus, the play refuses to stay still, fluttering past the nets and lime sticks of the critics. Instead of resisting this conclusion, we might try following the direction in which the birds of the *Birds* take us, plodding like the protagonists behind jackdaw and crow. Nor should someone object that a chorus is not a comedy, that plot, music, language count for more. Within the sociology of Athenian comedy in the fifth century B.C., the chorus is primary; the comic poet is most often identified not as a playwright but as the "teacher" of the chorus (*didaskalos*). The recruiting and payment for the twenty-four-member chorus (nonprofessionals, neighbors and friends of the audience) was a civic duty required of the wealthiest Athenians, but also a point of pride for these prominent citizens. Consequently, dramatic competition was to a large extent a matter of dueling choruses performing before fanatic hometown crowds.

Furthermore, within the poetics of Aristophanic comedy, the chorus is at the root of each play's idea, bonded by visual and verbal metaphor to the plots (such as they are), and expressing with brilliant dramatic conciseness the deeper theme. "Clouds," for example, embody the puffery, changeability, and pomposity of the character Socrates in that play; "wasps" nicely personify the venomous voting practices of Cleon's geriatric jurors. In each case, understanding the chorus-concept is the first step toward interpretation.

The concepts are not simple: this poet's art always balances a lyrical interiority (for choruses produce vivid *images* along with their varied associations) against a social exterior. On one hand, the existence of the chorus allows Aristophanes to dramatize problems in terms of *group* attitudes and reactions, as he analyzes the formation of opinion and the motivations for political movement. In this way, comedy made for a radically democratic art-form; not accidentally, Aristophanes' genre of Old Comedy (the type that was abusive, fantastic, with integrated choral roles) flourished while

Athens was an independent city state and declined after its defeat by Sparta in 404. The social nature of the chorus meant that it could represent recognized constituencies, such as the people of Acharnia and the "new class," or the disenfranchised, as in the "women"'s plays, *Lysistrata, Ecclesiazusae* (*Celebrating Ladies*), *Thesmophoriazusae* (*The Sexual Congress*). Even when the chorus represents birds, it is clearly an avian *community*, one that in this play comes to resemble a political audience, a crowd under the smooth-talking Peisetairus ("he who persuades a companion").

On the other hand, the lyrical side of the chorus, its resemblance to a pure image or an extended Homeric-style simile, must have directed an audience toward something more than social commentary, to nature rather than culture, if you like. In the case of the *Birds*, this feeling is reinforced because their choral persona fits their practical performance role on stage: all choruses sing and dance, but *birds* are, after all, naturals at the part. The classicist Gilbert Highet once remarked (apropos of birdwatching, not Aristophanes):

All men and women on earth take trouble to decorate their homes and their bodies and their equipment, whether such decoration consists of a few brass bowls or of a glittering Cadillac. These activities are artistic. The only other living beings on the planet which consistently engage in the same kind of activity are the birds.[1]

By extension, to write a play about birds is akin to making poetry about the *origins* of song and dance: it is "metapoetic" poetry. In Greek tradition, poets often affiliated themselves with birds; choral poetry always acknowledged a closeness to these natural sources of song. The Spartan poet Alkman, for instance, a composer of young women's choruses in the seventh century B.C., claimed, "I know the songs of all birds." This convention is taken to its extreme in airy-fairy dithyrambs of the type mocked by Aristophanes in *Birds*; it seems that by his time the trope of "the wings of song" had become tired and trite. Aristophanes' play revives the trope (the protagonists actually *become* birds by eating a magic root), but at the same time makes fun of it.

The tension is part of a larger movement embodied in the drama. In *Birds*

---

[1] *Talents and Geniuses* (New York: Meridian Books, 1959), p. 4.

it seems that the lyric, as I defined it above, is always tugging against the social. That is, the play celebrates the birdlike urge to sing, to dance, to eat whenever and whatever you can, and to procreate on the fly. The central portions of this play articulate a dream vision that is pure pleasure principle. Who would not want to soar away from lawyers and defecate on enemies? In this vision, the chorus are the heroes. What is more, they are convinced by Peisetairus that they are more divine than heroes, that their power is older and greater than that of the Olympian gods, that the real origin of earth began with the death of a father-bird rather than the rule of Father Zeus. The dream world of bird-power is thus simultaneously Utopia and Golden Age, an idyll of once and future kings. And we, like the chorus, are willing to be persuaded as well, because this lyric image of avian glory touches that lost green world of every adult's desires.

But the social, like a superego, keeps intruding on the id's idyll. Here the problematic of the play works out, to some extent, the dilemmas of democracy, a set of issues with which Athens was just coming to terms in its brief independent century. If Athenians, proud victors of the Persian Wars that ended in 479, most valued freedom (*eleutheria*) as a community, to what extent could individuals *within* the city state expect and value the same ideal? Or is it inevitable that to be human is to be (as Aristotle was to say in the next century) a "political animal," formed by and fitted best to the *polis*?

This social side of the *Birds* occludes the lyric, again and again. It suggests several ironies. First, there are those stemming from inherent national quirks, the comic counterpart of tragedy's inherited guilt: take two Athenians, send them to the jungle, and they'll always end up planning vast community improvement projects and passing a slew of laws. Second, there are ironies of history, with its ominous undertones in both myths and contemporary events. The Hoopoe, master of the birds, may seem to have flown from the nightmare of history, but his personal story would have been much on the minds of Athenians (since it was dramatized in at least two tragedies in the fifth century). Gory stuff, full of psychosexual and political implications. Tereus was formerly king of Thrace; he married Procne, daughter of Pandion, king of Athens, raped her sister Philomela, then cut out her tongue to cover up the deed. He was incriminated when Philomela wove the narrative of events into something like a tapestry, whereupon Procne took her revenge by murdering their son Itys. All three were turned to birds by the gods to end the violence: Tereus to a hoopoe, Philomela to a swallow, and Procne to a nightingale. The latter's beautiful song, so enchanting in this drama, may make us forget that its singer, in the world of myth, was a mother turned bird mourning her slain son.

A similar dark border frames the myth of the birds' sovereignty. Not only is it ironic that this defeat of the Olympian order of gods under Zeus is staged in a theater dedicated to his son Dionysus, in the presence of the god's priest. Fruitless threats to the eternal rule of Zeus were the subject of several works of art that any Athenian theater-goer would know: most prominently the victory of Zeus and his siblings against the Giants was depicted on the east side of the newly built Parthenon, just up the hill from the spot where spectators would have experienced the *Birds*. For all that one might want the birds to win, myth taught that such attempts were doomed.

Doomed too, as it turned out, was the huge Athenian military expedition that had sailed the summer before the *Birds* was produced, on its way to gain control of neutral Sicily in a strategic move designed to win the war against Sparta. By the time of the production the attack had not gone wrong; only in the next year would thousands of Athenians be annihilated at Syracuse, the rest imprisoned in quarries where they perished. Perhaps the play hinted to some members of the audience that an expanding Athenian empire presented such dangers, just as it may have suggested to others that Athens was rotting from the inside, a dystopia overrun by slick professional lecturers ("sophists"), vapid poets, rhetoricians, and sycophants.

While the critics still debate the exact relevance of this play to its social context, it remains clear that these darker elements of contemporary history did not completely overshadow the *Birds*. As cynically as one might read the play, the ironies never completely corrode the gleaming moments of utopic desire. Yet those moments never have the strength to overpower bleaker thoughts. The most horrific and the funniest coexist: Peisetairus rooks birds, then actually roasts his own adopted kin, but we laugh because the scene is nested within an old Heracles-the-glutton joke (like real Athenian gourmets, he savors bird meat). In this merciless, vertiginous ambiguity the play's true wisdom resides.

It might stem from the cultural ambivalence of Greeks toward birds themselves, creatures who were, in their terms, both stupid and wise. "Birdbrain" is an insult Greeks would understand: the famous "ode to man" in Sophocles' *Antigone*, a key text for Athenian self-definition in mid-fifth century, praises human ability to tame the ox, the earth, and "the races of empty-minded birds." On the other hand, to a Greek birds were undoubtedly mysterious conveyors of divine messages and power: the eagle of Zeus, owl of Athena, peacock of Hera, and Aphrodite's sparrow were real presences. Like snakes, who were fed at shrines, birds were thought to have secret access to a part of the universe humans could not attain. Hence the double vision. A city of birds might be as absurd as a conspiracy of squirrels; their tiny brains can hold only enough for the day; they cannot scheme, debate, orate—all the things at which Athenians are expert. But birds always seem happier than humans; they must know something we cannot—perhaps that intellect is not everything.

It is the genius of Aristophanes to have tapped into this deep ambiguity in creating his chorus and the play shaped around it. He melds the optimism of the lyric poet to the pessimism of a social critic. A lesser poet may have produced a less ambiguous play by abandoning one or the other mood. Aristophanes, however, had the ability ascribed to first-rate intelligence by another elegiac critic, F. Scott Fitzgerald, in *The Crack-Up*: to hold two diametrically opposed views in the mind at once and not go mad.

Any critique of thematics, plot functions, and character must resign itself to looking feeble beside comedy itself. Alongside the intellectual acuity of Aristophanes runs the manic energy of his productions. Think of Punch and Judy. Sprinkle in *Mad Magazine* and *Saturday Night Live*. Add a few fast cartoons—not genteel contemporary ones about talking bees and ponies, but the fantastic old Road Runner and Bugs Bunny variety. Throw in some striptease and vaudeville, some British music hall patter songs, dabs of Gilbert and Sullivan, a dash of Chaplin, Monty Python galore, some great duos (Abbott and Costello, Laurel and Hardy), and a few solo acts (Harold Lloyd, Fatty Arbuckle). It's still not as good as Aristophanes. But maybe the whole mix comes close. And to my mind this new translation by Paul Muldoon captures the whole thing—madness, lyricism, acidity—accurately and with brilliance.

NOTE ON THE TEXT AND FURTHER READING

In assisting the translator, I have generally followed the text and notes of Dunbar's recent edition, preferring in some places the reading and interpretations of others, chiefly Sommerstein. The following books and articles offer the interested reader wider perspectives on the play and further bibliography.

Bowie, A. M. *Aristophanes: Myth, Ritual, and Comedy.* Cambridge and New York: Cambridge University Press.

Dobrov, Gregory W., ed. *The City as Comedy: Society and Representation in Athenian Drama.* Chapel Hill: University of North Carolina Press, 1995.

Dunbar, Nan, ed. *Aristophanes, Birds.* Oxford and New York: Clarendon Press, 1995.

Hubbard, Thomas K. *The Masks of Comedy: Aristophanes and the Intertextual Parabasis.* Ithaca, N.Y.: Cornell University Press, 1995.

MacDowell, Douglas M. *Aristophanes and Athens: An Introduction to the Plays.* Oxford and New York: Oxford University Press, 1995.

Pozzi, Dora. "The Pastoral Ideal in *The Birds* of Aristophanes." *Classical Journal* 82, 3 (1986): 119–29.

Russo, Carlo Ferdinando. *Aristophanes, an Author for the Stage.* Trans. Kevin Wren. London and New York: Routledge, 1994.

Segal, Erich, ed. *Oxford Readings in Aristophanes.* Oxford and New York: Oxford University Press, 1996.

Sommerstein, Alan H., ed. and trans. *Birds.* Warminster, Wiltshire: Aris and Phillips, 1987.

Cast

EUELPIDES, a citizen of Athens
PEISETAIROS, another citizen
XANTHIAS, a slave
MANES, another slave
MERGANSERVANT, assistant to the Hoopoe
HOOPOE, once the human Tereus
CHORUS of twenty-four birds
CHORUS LEADER
PRIEST
BARD
ORACLE MONGER
METON, a mathematician
STATUTE SELLER
OMBIRDSMAN
FIRST RUNNER
SECOND RUNNER
RAINBOW, a manifestation of Iris
THIRD RUNNER
BIRDNIK
KINESIAS, a poet
SUPERGROUSE
PROMETHEUS, a demigod
POSEIDON, god of the sea
HERACLES, a demigod
GOD OF THE TRIBALLIANS
HEAVENLY RUNNER
NONSPEAKING
    Various birds
    Hoopoe's servants
    Chairis, a piper
    Nightingale, once Procne wife of Tereus
    Queen Maybe, a bride-to-be

(A wooded, rocky landscape. Two Athenians, Euelpides and
    Peisetairos, clamber onto the stage. They wear the masks of old

*men. Euelpides leads, or is led by, a pet jackdaw, Peisetairos a
crow on a string. They are followed by two slaves, Xanthias and
Manes, loaded down with luggage—baskets, pots, bedding.)*

EUELPIDES *(to his jackdaw)*
> Let me get this straight? We should be aiming for that tree? No?
> That tree up ahead?

PEISETAIROS *(to the jackdaw)*
> I'll have your guts for garters.
(points to the crow)
>> Now this one's saying "Baaaack, baaaaack."

EUELPIDES *(to Peisetairos)*
> You hopeless hoor. You gomeril. You glipe. I've had enough of
>> this wandering back and forth. I'm completely
>> wiped out. Totally whacked.

PEISETAIROS
> What about me? Following a crow all over the shop?

EUELPIDES
> While I'm at the mercy of a jackdaw, hirpling and hobbling
>> about wherever it happens to hop.

PEISETAIROS
> Now I haven't a baldy notion of our whereabouts in this great
>> world. You, no doubt, could find your way back
>> to Athens.

EUELPIDES
> Heavens, no. Not even Exekestides could get out of this. Even he
>> couldn't find his way back to the paternal perch.

PEISETAIROS *(groaning as he climbs)*
Hoooooooolyshi . . .

EUELPIDES
Listen, old son. That's nothing compared to the way *I* came. Why don't you try taking the *high* road to ruin?

PEISETAIROS
That Philokrates . . . Back in the bird-market . . . That black-biled byblow really hoodwinked us. He gave us to believe that the pair of *them*   10
(gestures to the crow and jackdaw)
would lead the pair of *us* straight to Tereus, the Hoopoe of all hoopoes. He sold us that blabbermouthed son of Tharreleides, that there jackdaw, for one obol and this here crow for *three* obols. It turns out they're good for nothing but biting.
(to the jackdaw)
What are you gawking at now? You're not going to lead us straight into the face of the cliff? There's no way we're going through there.

EUELPIDES
It's a no-go area. A no through road.
(The crow begins to cackle and caw.)

PEISETAIROS
The crow here . . . About the road . . . She's saying something . . . She seems to be changing her tune.

EUELPIDES
How's that? What's she saying? Can you make her out?

PEISETAIROS
Only that . . .
(The crow pauses, then cackles and caws even more raucously.)
she's going to cut my hand off at the wrist.

EUELPIDES *(addressing the audience directly)*
>Isn't this just terrific? Here you have a situation where two people
>>actually want to get to hell out of Athens. We get
>>ourselves all fitted and kitted out with the bags
>>and baskets and . . . then what? We lose our way.
>The fact of the matter, ladies and gentlemen, is that here we have
>>a problem not unlike the famous Akestor's,
>>though arse-about-face. Akestor, being a
>>foreigner, was looking for a way *in*. We're fully
>>paid up members of the club, Athenians of good
>>standing, and we're clearing *out*, flying the coop.
>It's not as if we're being shooed off, either. It's not even as if
>>we don't like the city, that we don't accept its
>>intrinsic greatness. Isn't it as grand a spot as a
>>body might find—if you like being *fined*, that
>>is. If you like paying summonses.
>The grasshoppers restrict themselves to chittering away in the fig-
>>trees for a month, maybe two, out of twelve. The
>>citizens of Athens chitter and witter on in the
>>courts of law year in, year out.   20
>That's why we've taken to the road, with our sacrificial basket
>>and sacrificial cooking pot and our myrtle
>>branches for sacrificial garlands. We're looking
>>for a place that's trouble-free. A place where we
>>might settle and live our lives in peace.
>That's why we're looking for Tereus, the Hoopoe of all
>>hoopoes. Maybe he'll be able to tell us if, in all
>>his flights of fancy, he's come upon such a place.

PEISETAIROS
>Hey . . .

EUELPIDES
>What gives?

PEISETAIROS
>The crow keeps gaping at something up there.

EUELPIDES

The jackdaw, too. Trying to tell us something, I suspect. I bet you the place is coming down with birds. We'll know for sure if we raise a bit of a rumpus.
(They stop before a smooth cliff-face. Euelpides hits the rock with his foot.)

PEISETAIROS

That's the idea. Kick the rock and the birds will flock.

EUELPIDES

You bang it with your head. It'll make twice as much noise.

PEISETAIROS

Uh huh. Use a stone.

EUELPIDES

Whatever you say.
(bangs on the cliff-face)
Hey, you boy, you.

PEISETAIROS

"You boy, you"? Are you out of your tree? You call the Hoopoe "You boy, you"?

EUELPIDES

Hoopoe . . . You're going to make me knock again? Hoopoe . . .   30
(The Merganservant appears from the cliff-face. He wears a horrendous bird-mask. The crow and jackdaw flap away, followed by the slaves.)

MERGANSERVANT

Who crows there? Who wishes an audience with His Excellency?

EUELPIDES *(terrified)*

In the name of all that's holy. Would you look at the trap on this one?

MERGANSERVANT

Jeeeeeeeeeeeeepers Creeeeeeeeeepers. If it isn't a pair of bird-
catchers.

EUELPIDES

I don't like the sound of this.

MERGANSERVANT

Would you people go take a running jump.

EUELPIDES

Never fear. We're not people. Not real people.

MERGANSERVANT

You're not? What are you then?

EUELPIDES

I myself am a wary . . .

MERGANSERVANT

A *wary*? You mean a cassowary?

EUELPIDES

No. I mean a Veryverywary . . . a Libyan bird . . .   40

MERGANSERVANT

You're talking gibberish.
(to Peisetairos)

And what kind of bird are you?

PEISETAIROS

Can't you tell just by looking at my feet? I'm a Greater Spotted
Poopoe.

EUELPIDES

And you? What are you when you're at home?

MERGANSERVANT *(drawing himself up)*
I myself have the honor of being a Merganservant.

EUELPIDES
A Merganservant? So you threw in the towel to some
Merganmaster?

MERGANSERVANT
No, but when His Excellency was converted into a hoopoe, he
entreated that I become a bird also, so that he
might have an acolyte or deacon. Someone to
oversee.

EUELPIDES
A bird needs someone to do for him?

MERGANSERVANT
The Hoopoe does. Probably because he was once a human. So
that, now, when he has a hankering for some
fresh sardines, I take off with my jar to Phaleron
for some fresh sardines. Or he'll want a drop of
soup, I go fetch the ladle and soup tureen.

PEISETAIROS
So you're what you might call a Campfowler. I tell you what,
Campfowler . . . why don't you let His Eminence
know we're here?

MERGANSERVANT
That I can't do just now. He's taking a nap after a spot of lunch.
A light repast of myrtleberries and gnats.   50

PEISETAIROS
Give him a clarion call in any case.

MERGANSERVANT
He'll not be too pleased about having his beauty sleep
interrupted by the likes of you two.
(The Merganservant disappears into the cliff-face.)

PEISETAIROS *(calling after)*
Bad cess to you, for scaring the shit out of me.

EUELPIDES
He scared the shit out of my jackdaw, too.

PEISETAIROS
I think you mean that he scared the shit out of *you* and *you* let
the jackdaw get away, yellowbelly.

EUELPIDES
And what about you? *You* let the crow go.

PEISETAIROS
Go? No.

EUELPIDES
Where is she, so, you pill?

PEISETAIROS
She went away of her own free will.

EUELPIDES
Her own free will? Aren't you the gallant galoot?   60

HOOPOE *(booming from within)*
Open the door. I'm coming out.
*(The Hoopoe steps out. He's a somewhat dowdy figure despite black and
white barred wings, a resplendent crest, a sharply
hooked beak.)*

EUELPIDES

Heavens above. Just look at the cut of that. The crest . . . the
rest . . .

HOOPOE

Who are you who seek me?

PEISETAIROS

The twelve gods . . .
(The Hoopoe looks askance.)
seem to have played their part in togging you out.

HOOPOE

You fellows aren't pulling my leg because of my regimentals, I
hope. I was, after all, a military man.

EUELPIDES

We're not laughing at *you* as such.

HOOPOE

What's so funny, then?

EUELPIDES

The beak seems a bit much.

HOOPOE

But that's exactly how Sophocles portrays me in his tragedy about
Tereus.

EUELPIDES

So you're Tereus. Are you a common or garden bird, or some
kind of exotic thing, a peacock maybe?   70

HOOPOE

A bird, of course.

EUELPIDES
    What's happened to all your fancy feathers?

HOOPOE
    They fell out, I'm afraid.

EUELPIDES
    From some distemper?

HOOPOE
    No. All birds lose their plumage in the wintertime.
    Then we grow new ones. But tell me this. Who are you?

PEISETAIROS
    Us? We're humans.

HOOPOE
    Humans of what stripe? What class of humans?

PEISETAIROS
    We come from a notable ship-building town.

HOOPOE
    You're not jurymen, by any chance?   80

PEISETAIROS
    Exactly. *Not*jurymen.

HOOPOE
    What seed or breed would that be?

EUELPIDES
    You can still find them in the countryside, if you cast your
                net wide enough, though they're few and far
            between.

HOOPOE
    What brings you to this neck of the woods?

PEISETAIROS
    We want your advice.

HOOPOE
    On what?

PEISETAIROS
    Well, you were once human like us and, like us, you once owed
            money and, like us, you didn't like to pay it back.
            Then you turned into a bird. You flew over land
            and sea, you got an overall view of things from
            the unique perspective of a bird-man. That's why
            we've come for your advice.
    Maybe you could direct us to a city where things are a bit
            better . . . where life's a bit . . . cushier.

HOOPOE
    You're looking for a city better than Athens?

PEISETAIROS
    Not *better* . . . Just somewhere where life isn't quite so hard.   90

HOOPOE
    Somewhere run by people with a sense of a pedigree? By the local
            aristocracy?

EUELPIDES
    Not at all. The very idea of that Aristokrates person makes me
            want to throw up.

HOOPOE
    What sort of city do you have in mind?

EUELPIDES

It would be a place where a really bad day would begin with some neighbor knocking on your door and issuing you with a summons, "Would you for heaven's sake come over to my place after you've had your bath. Bring the children too. I'm having a wedding feast and I'm charging you to appear there. I'll be mortified if you don't attend."

HOOPOE

So you like a hard time.
(to Peisetairos)

What's your take on this?

PEISETAIROS

That's what I'm after, too.

HOOPOE

You're after what exactly?

PEISETAIROS

I'm after a situation in which a man comes up to me, red in the face with anger. He's the father of a pretty young boy. "Wasn't that nice of you," he says. "You meet my son on the way back from the gym after a bath. You don't kiss him. You don't speak to him. You don't embrace him. You don't even tickle his balls. And to think that our families have been friends since forever."

HOOPOE

You're pathetic. That you'd want to give yourself such a hard time. But I do believe there's a city offering something along these lines. It's on the Arabian sea.

EUELPIDES

    Not on the sea, if you don't mind. Before we knew it the
           Salaminia would be putting in with some
           Athenian official issuing a warrant for something
           or other . . . Isn't there somewhere inland in
           Greece itself?   100

HOOPOE

    What about putting down roots in Lepreon?

EUELPIDES

    No thanks. I've never set foot in the place, but I have laid eyes
           on their scabby poet, Melanthios. He's leprous
           enough for me.

HOOPOE

    What about settling in Opous with the Opuntians?

EUELPIDES

    And be known as "Opountios" like that one-eyed old son-of-
           a-snitch. Not for a crock of gold. I'm thinking,
           though, of what it must be like to live here with
           the birds. How do you find it here yourself?

HOOPOE

    It's not a bad place to spend some time. To begin with, we don't
           carry wallets.

EUELPIDES

    So you don't have to deal with all that's counterfeit in life.

HOOPOE

    We move from little tufted spot to spot, nibbling on white
           sesame and myrtle berries and poppy and
           water-mint.

EUELPIDES
You lead the life of newlyweds, in other words.

PEISETAIROS *(abruptly)*
I've just had a vision of what life might be like for you birds, of
how you really might rule the roost, if you were
to follow my suggestions.

HOOPOE
Suggestions on what?   110

PEISETAIROS
My first suggestion would be that you give up this business of
flying around aimlessly all day with your beak
hanging open. It doesn't show you in a good
light. Where we come from, if you ask about
Theogenes, say, someone like Teleas will
immediately describe him as "a bird-brain,
fluttering, flapping, flighty, footloose, incapable
of staying still from moment to moment."

HOOPOE
I think I see what you're getting at. What, then, do you
recommend as our course of action?

PEISETAIROS
You must set up a city.

HOOPOE
Birds set up a city? How can birds set up a city?

PEISETAIROS
That's a stupid question, if I may say so. Just look down here.

HOOPOE
I'm looking.

PEISETAIROS
   Now look up there.

HOOPOE
   I'm looking.

PEISETAIROS
   Try turning around.

HOOPOE *(straining)*
   This is just great. I'm going to wring my own neck.   120

PEISETAIROS
   What do you see?

HOOPOE
   I see the clouds. Cirrus. Cumulus. The clouds and the sky.

PEISETAIROS
   And isn't that the province of the birds?
   Isn't that their *polis*?

HOOPOE
   Polis in what sense?

PEISETAIROS
   In the sense of both the "city state" of the birds and the "pole"
           or "axis" around which the heavens move. If we
           were to throw up a "pale" around the "pole"
           then we'd have our "polis." On one hand, the
           birds would set themselves above the humans
           just as humans set themselves above
           grasshoppers. On the other, we'd shut out the
           gods. We'd cut them off just as we cut off the
           Melians when we laid siege to them. They'd
           starve to death.

HOOPOE
How so?

PEISETAIROS
You know how the air comes between the gods and the earth.
You know how we have to ask the Boeotians for
safe passage whenever we want to go to Delphi.
It'll be just the same for the gods. If the gods
don't pay you an annual tribute, you won't allow
people to make sacrifices to them. You won't
allow the smoke of burnt offerings in your air
space.

HOOPOE
Knock me down with a feather! By all the traps, meshes, and
mist-nets in the universe, I've never heard a
cleverer idea. I myself would like to help you
set up this city, so long as the other birds are
in accord.

PEISETAIROS
Who's going to put the case to them?   130

HOOPOE
You may do that yourself. I've been with them for so long now
they've all learned the lingo. Before that they
spoke some heathen gobbledygook.

PEISETAIROS
How do you call them all together, though?

HOOPOE
Simple. I'll just head into the bush there and rouse my
nightingale and we'll put out the word. When
they hear both of us they'll come as fast as
they can.
(The Hoopoe climbs up through the overgrown rock face.)

PEISETAIROS *(delighting in the possibility for double-entendres)*
> That's it. Get a move on. You "head into the bush" and "rouse"
> > your—what do you call it?—your "nightingale."
(The Hoopoe has clambered onto the top of the cliff-face and sings out
> > *from his vantage point.)*

HOOPOE
> Come, my darling. Time to stir yourself.
> From your holy mouth
> pour forth your holy hymns.
> For our late-lamented son, Itys, let there come
> from your vibrant throat
> those vibrant notes   140
> of grief that twist and intertwine
> through the leafy bryony-vine
> till they find their way up to the very
> throne of Zeus where Phoebus, lifting his ivory-
> bound lyre, plays in response.
> Then the gods will begin to dance
> and your ochones and ullagones
> be given back in the cry of those Blessed Ones.
(A flute stands in for the nightingale.)

EUELPIDES
> What a beautiful voice that bird has. Her voice has drenched the
> > thicket in . . . honey.

PEISETAIROS
> Hey.   150

EUELPIDES
> What?

PEISETAIROS
> Why don't you shut your beak?

EUELPIDES
How come?

PEISETAIROS
The Hoopoe is getting ready to sing in his turn.

HOOPOE *(again singing out loud and clear)*
Epopopoi popopoi popoi
Tra la tra la tra la tra la tra
Ladies and gentlemen of the feathered classes,
the time has come to get off your asses
and leave the farmer's seeded acres.
All you who count as corn-pickers   160
and barley-eaters.
All you who fill the furrow's amphitheater
with your trills and twitters
of tio tio tio tio tio tio tio tio.
All you who live in the high pastures
and browse on ivy, oleaster
and arbutus, the time has come to leave the sticks
for my trioto trioto totobrix.
All you who live by the moors and marshy ditches
on mosquitoes and man-eating midges.   170
All you who run upon
the watery meadows of Marathon,
which accounts in part for the meaty shins
of black partridges, also known as francolins.
All of you who have a taste
for the halcyon days on the watery waste,
the time has come to foregather
to hear the latest news and weather.
There's a change in the air.
Come and listen to this cute hoor.   180
He's full of bright ideas he's intent
on bodying out, for he has quite a practical bent.
So come on over, if you would.

Toro toro toro torotix.
Kikkabau. Kikkabau.
Toro toro toro toro lililix.

PEISETAIROS
I see no birds. Do you?

EUELPIDES
Not a cheep.

PEISETAIROS
It seems as if His Excellency is wasting his breath, wheeping there
like a whimbrel.

HOOPOE
Torotix. Torotix.   190

PEISETAIROS
Look here. Here comes something. Some class of a bird.
(A flamingo minces in.)

EUELPIDES
It's a bird, okay. But what? A peacock, maybe?

PEISETAIROS
Let's ask His Worship.
(to the Hoopoe)
                    What's this when it's at home?

HOOPOE
This isn't one of your run of the mill birds. This is a wader of
some kind. A bottom feeder.

PEISETAIROS
Nice one. Nice and red.

HOOPOE
>   You've hit the nail on the head. That's why he's known as a Red
>   Ding Nutscratch.

EUELPIDES
>   Watch out.

PEISETAIROS
>   What are you shouting about?

EUELPIDES
>   Here comes another one.
>   *(A rooster enters.)*

PEISETAIROS
>   "Another" is right. How weird can you get? This is a fateful bird,
>   if I'm not mistaken.   200
>   *(to Hoopoe)*
>   What's the story with this strange, high-stepping fellow?

HOOPOE
>   This is a Persian fowl . . .

PEISETAIROS
>   A foul Persian? Lord above. Where did he park his camel?
>   *(A second hoopoe enters.)*

EUELPIDES
>   And this? This one has a crest.

PEISETAIROS
>   Would you credit that? So you're not the only Hoopoe in the
>   world.

HOOPOE
>   This is a son of the one in the play by Philokles, and I'm his
>   grandfather. It's like when you recycle names

like "Hipponikus MacKallias" and, in the next
generation, "Kallias MacHipponikus."

PEISETAIROS
This is a plain Kalli-ass, I'd say, from the way he's molting.

HOOPOE
That's because he's so well-bred he gets stripped of everything
by his hangers-on. Anything that's left is plucked
out by the womenfolk.

EUELPIDES
Hoooooooolysh . . . Here comes some yellow-bellied bird. Looks
like he's dyed-in-the-wool.
(The greater gorb enters.)

HOOPOE
This is a Greater Gorb.   210

PEISETAIROS
The only gorb I know of is that greedy Kleonymos creature.

EUELPIDES
How come he hasn't thrown down his helmet and shield and run
like hell?

PEISETAIROS
How come these birds are all wearing crests? Are they going to
run a double-lap in full battle-gear?

HOOPOE
Not at all. No. They live on the crests of hills, like the Carians. It's
safer up there.
*(The flamingo, rooster, second hoopoe, and greater gorb dance together
before moving off.)*

PEISETAIROS
>Jeeeeeeeeepers Creeeeeeeepers. Look at this slew of birds.
>*(The Chorus of twenty-four birds flutters in along the ramps to a dancing
>area.)*

EUELPIDES
>Hoooooooooooooooly Mooooooooooooooly. What a shower. You
>can't see the boards for birds.

PEISETAIROS
>A partridge.

EUELPIDES
>A francolin.

PEISETAIROS
>A widgeon.

EUELPIDES
>A halcyon. And behind her?   220

HOOPOE
>A permagain.

EUELPIDES
>There's no such bird as a permagain.

HOOPOE
>What about Sporgilos the hairdresser? He'd give you a
>permagain. If it isn't an owl.

PEISETAIROS
>Bringing owls to Athens. That's one for the books.

HOOPOE
>Just take a gander at this. Jay, turtle dove, lark, warbler,
>stonechat, rock dove, vulture, falcon, wood dove,

cuckoo, red shank, goldfinch, moorhen, kestrel,
grebe, waxwing, lammergeier, woodpecker.

PEISETAIROS

What a racket. All blethering and blaring. Are they after us, do
you think? They certainly seem to be taking quite
an interest in us.

EUELPIDES

It sure looks that way.

CHORUS

Whereabababababababababouts is the bird
who sent out the word?
Whawhawhawhat is his present location?   230

HOOPOE

That would be me. I'm here.

CHORUS

Can you give some sense
of the lalalalalalalatest intelligence
to the assesesesesesembled bird-nation?

HOOPOE

I have to make an important announcement that impinges on all
of us. It has to do with something both sweet and
useful. These two wise men have made their way
to me.

CHORUS

Whowhowho? Whawhawhat? Whewhewhere?

HOOPOE

The fact is that these two human beings have come among us
with an earth-shattering idea.

CHORUS LEADER
>Human beings? You brought us human beings? Not since I flew
>>the nest have I come across such a case of the
>>headstaggers.

HOOPOE
>There's nothing to bother your head about.

CHORUS LEADER
>What have you gone and done?   240

HOOPOE
>I've decided to welcome two men who wanted to get together
>>with us.

CHORUS LEADER
>You have, haven't you?

HOOPOE
>I have, and I stand by my decision.

CHORUS LEADER
>Are they in the immediate vicinity?

HOOPOE
>As surely as I am myself.

CHORUS LEADER
>My fellow birds, we've been betrayed.
>We've fallen into a trap laid
>by a supposed friend who fed with the rest
>of us in the fields. Now he's transgressed
>the oaths and ordinances of birds.   250
>The Hoopoe has lured
>us into the toils of those
>godless ones who've been our mortal foes

since time began. We'll deal with him
in due course. Let's tear these ones limb from limb.

PEISETAIROS

Uh oh. Looks like our goose is cooked.

EUELPIDES

It's all your fault. Why did you have to bring me with you?

PEISETAIROS

So you'd have someone to follow.

EUELPIDES

So I might weep bitter tears.

PEISETAIROS

Would you ever give over? There'll be no weeping for you, in any
            event. They'll have pecked out your eyes. You
            need eyes to weep.   260

CHORUS

Yo yo.
Onward and upward. Sound the attack.
Pin their arms behind their backs.
Surround them. Let them shiver
in fear. We'll soon be eating their livers.
No shady hill nor cloud nor sea
shall offer them immunity.

CHORUS LEADER

Come on. Let's pluck their skinny shanks.
Where's the line-commander? Bring up the right flank.

EUELPIDES

Time to walk the chalks.   270

PEISETAIROS
What's your hurry?

EUELPIDES
I don't want to be torn apart by these ones.

PEISETAIROS
How exactly do you plan to make your escape?

EUELPIDES
I haven't a clue.
(Peisetairos rummages among their possessions.)

PEISETAIROS
I tell you what. Let's take a couple of these pots and baking
bowls.

EUELPIDES
What use is a bowl going to be?

PEISETAIROS
No waking owl comes near a baking bowl.

EUELPIDES
What about those sharp-clawed ones?

PEISETAIROS
Here, take this spit and brandish it in front of you.   280

EUELPIDES
And our eyes?

PEISETAIROS
Cover them with a saucer.

EUELPIDES

Aren't you as clever as all get out? A born field marshal. You leave
Nicias in the shade.

CHORUS LEADER

Eleleu.
Level your beaks and charge.
Begin by breaking that baking-bowl targe.

HOOPOE

Come to your senses. What do you mean by attacking two men
who are kith and kin to my own good wife?

CHORUS

Should we show them more mercy than we would two wolves?
Could we find anything more hostile than themselves?

HOOPOE

They may be enemies by nature, but they've come here as
friends. They've come to teach us something
useful.

CHORUS LEADER

How could they ever teach us something useful? These are our
enemies from the dawn of time.   290

HOOPOE

But isn't it from their enemies that the wise learn? The idea of
"Better safe than sorry," for example. That's not
something you'd learn from a friend. With an
enemy, you learn it right off. It's from their
enemies that city states learn to build high walls
and strengthen their naval defenses. That's how
they protect their families, homes, and wealth.

CHORUS LEADER

Maybe we should listen to them first. We learn from our
enemies, as you so rightly put it.

PEISETAIROS

They've calmed down a smidgin. Fall back, one step at a time.

HOOPOE

It's only right and proper that you pay attention to me. You're in
my debt.

CHORUS LEADER

We've never gone against you, have we?

PEISETAIROS

They're being quite unthreatening, in fact. Put down the pot and
saucers. Hold on to the spit, though. We'll need
that to patrol the battlements. Keep an eye out
over the top of the pot.
(They crouch behind the pot.)
There's no way we can make a run for it.

EUELPIDES

If we do happen to hop the twig, where will we be buried?

PEISETAIROS

In the Potters' Fields, it goes without saying. If we want to be
buried by the state we'll have to tell the generals
we fought at the battle of the Yellow Bird.

CHORUS LEADER

Back in line. As you were.   300
Practice a little self-restraint.
Let's hear such views
as this pair might share
with us. Let's hear what they want.
Hey, Hoopoe. I'm talking to you.

HOOPOE

What do you want to know?

CHORUS LEADER

Who are these boys? Where are they from?

HOOPOE

They're from the so-called "Athens of the north." A seat of
    learning.

CHORUS LEADER

So why are they away with the birds?

HOOPOE

They wish to meet with you and get to know, in an intimate way,
    how you live. They want to be . . . intimate with
    you.   310

CHORUS LEADER

How do you mean? Has that boy been bending your ear?

HOOPOE

Only with unbelievable stuff. Wonderful stuff.

CHORUS LEADER

What's he got to gain by hanging out with us? Some advantage
    to his friends? Some disadvantage to his foes?
    What's in it for him?

HOOPOE

He'll be bringing you news of an extraordinary bit of good
    fortune that can come your way. It can be yours,
    all of it, always.

CHORUS LEADER

He must have a slate loose.

HOOPOE
>Not at all.

CHORUS LEADER
>He's got to be one sandwich short of a picnic.

HOOPOE
>He's the model of sanity, I promise you. He's resourceful,
>>purposeful, guileful, everythingful.

CHORUS LEADER
>Let's hear what the old coot has to say? You've got me all worked
>>up now.

HOOPOE *(calling to his two servants)*
>Come and gather up all this decommissioned material and put it
>>away in the kitchen near the pot-stand.   320
>*(The servants enter and gather up the pots and pans. The Hoopoe turns
>>to Peisetairos.)*
>Now you explain to them why I've brought them here.

PEISETAIROS
>Me? Not unless they swear a solemn oath—the kind the
>>monkey-man swore to his knife-grinder wife—
>>not to bite me or twist my balls or poke me in
>>the . . .
>*(The chorus leader points to his ass.)*
>No, poke me in the *eyes*.

CHORUS LEADER
>We do most solemnly swear.

PEISETAIROS
>Swear it properly.

CHORUS
> We swear not to poke out this boy's eyes
> on condition that we win first prize
> by a unanimous vote of both audience and judges.

PEISETAIROS
> So shall it be.

CHORUS
> But if I break my vow, I'll win by a single vote.   330

HOOPOE *(to his two servants)*
> Attention. The heavy brigades should now retreat and await
>> further orders to be posted on the noticeboard.

CHORUS
> Though mankind has almost always been unkind
> and cunning and full of cant
> we have to admit
> that we're birdwits
> compared to you. So let's hear what you find,
> with your superior mind,
> to be the case.

CHORUS LEADER
> Hold nothing back.
> We won't be launching an attack.   340
> We won't be calling off the cease-fire.

PEISETAIROS
> I'm ready when you are. I've mixed all the ingredients of my
>> speech into one lump of dough and all it's
>> needing now is a little *kneading*. Bring me
>> my bay-crown and some water.

EUELPIDES
> Sounds like grub's up. Is it dinner-time?

PEISETAIROS
> No. I've been waiting for ages to make a major statement,
> > something with a bit of beef in it, that will
> > really knock their socks off.
> *(He pours water over his hands, puts on the orator's wreath, composes*
> > *himself.)*
> How I grieve for you, my dear birds. You who once were kings.

CHORUS
> Kings? Of what?

. PEISETAIROS
> Of all creation. You lorded it over me, him, over Zeus himself.
> > Before Cronus and the Titans, before the earth
> > itself, you were.

CHORUS LEADER
> Before the earth?

PEISETAIROS
> Sure.

CHORUS LEADER
> That's a new one on me.   350

PEISETAIROS
> You've obviously not read your Aesop. According to him, the
> > lark was the first of the birds. She existed before
> > the earth. When her father died from illness
> > there was no earth in which to bury him. He was
> > laid out for four days. Then, totally at a loss, she
> > hit on the idea of burying her father inside her
> > own head.

EUELPIDES

    That's what you call a "park in the lark."

PEISETAIROS

    It goes without saying that if you predated the gods and the earth
            itself then you have sovereignty over everything.

EUELPIDES

    You'd better keep your beaks well-honed, though. Zeus won't be
            likely to give up his scepter to some woodpecker,
            especially if it's been poking holes in his sacred
            oak-boles.

PEISETAIROS

    There's a wealth of evidence to suggest that birds were cocks of
            the walk in the old days. First of all, there's the
            example of the Cock himself, who ruled the
            Persians with an iron hand long before the likes
            of Darius and Megabazus. That's why he's still
            known as a Persian.

EUELPIDES

    That's why he's the only bird with such a tall crown, like a Persian
            king's.

PEISETAIROS

    So powerful was he then that even now he has it within him,
            when he starts up at dawn, to make everyone
            jump to attention and look lively—bronze-
            smiths, potters, tanners, cobblers, bath-
            attendants, barley-sellers and wood-turners who
            can make anything from a lyre to a shield. He
            can make them leap up, put on their sandals,
            and go out even while it's still pitch-black.

EUELPIDES

Tell me about it. I lost a good Phrygian cloak, unfortunately, on account of a cock. I'd been invited to a dinner party to celebrate the naming of some child and was having a gargle beforehand in town. When I got to the party I dozed off. The dinner hadn't even started when a cock crew and I assumed it was time to get up and start out for Alimos, which I did.

Just as I set foot outside the city wall, didn't a footpad give me a skite over the head with an ash-plant and leave me out for the count. I didn't even have a chance to cry out for help before he relieved me of my cloak.

PEISETAIROS

The kite was king of the Greeks in those days.   360

CHORUS

King of the Greeks? Of what do you speak?

PEISETAIROS

That's when the custom of paying homage to kites first appeared.

EUELPIDES

By all that's holy, I myself threw myself down on the ground once when I saw a kite. As I lay there on the flat of my back I swallowed the obol I was carrying in my mouth. I went home stony broke. Completely skint.

PEISETAIROS

It was the cuckoo, meanwhile, that ruled the roost in Egypt and Phoenicia. Whenever he called out "cuckoo," the Phoenicians would grab hold of their choppers and set out into the country to do their best endeavors in harvesting some marshy little field.

EUELPIDES
I see . . . So what he was really saying was, "Cuckoo, cuckoo . . .
    choppers to the *cuntry* . . ." No?

PEISETAIROS *(ignoring him)*
So dominant were birds in those days that even when
    Agamemnon or Menelaus became king a bird
    continued to perch on their royal scepters and
    got a share of any, you know, *donation* they
    received.

EUELPIDES
That I did not know. Though I was always taken aback when
    Priam would appear in one of those old tragedies
    with a bird. I see now he'd be watching out for
    any *donation* Lysicrates might be getting.

PEISETAIROS
The most striking thing of all is that Zeus, who is now first
    among the gods, always carries an eagle on his
    head. His daughter, Athena, carries an owl and
    Apollo, his attendant, a hawk.

CHORUS LEADER
By heavens, you're absolutely right. What's the reason, if I might?

PEISETAIROS
Simple. When someone's making a sacrifice and is offering up
    the roasted guts, as is usually the case, the bird
    can get to the guts before Zeus. Back then no one
    would swear by a god, you see, but by a bird.
    Even now the soothsayer, Lampon, swears an
    oath by a graylag goose when he's up to no good.
    There you have it.   370
Once you were held in high esteem, great and holy. Now they
    treat you as gomerils and glipes, as wee slavies,
    throwing stones at loons as if they were loonies.

Even inside the holy places they hunt you down
with nooses, snares, birdlime, mist-nets, trawl-
nets, and deadfalls.
When they catch you they sell you by the dozen. The people
buying you feel you up, of course, and, if they
decide you meet their standards, they don't just
roast you, plain and simple. They have to grate
cheese over you, cover you with oil, vinegar and
silphium, or some sickly-sweet, greasy sauce, as
if you were roadkill.

CHORUS
You've gone straight to the heart of the matter.
I weep to think of how our forefathers
let our birthright go by the board.
But you have come to save the birds.
I for one will entrust myself and all my cheeping
offspring to you for safekeeping.
You must tell us, though, what part we should play
to help carry the day.   380
Now our lives won't be worth living unless we can
restore our sovereignty. So what's the plan?

PEISETAIROS
First of all, there should be one bird city. That should be enclosed
with big, baked bricks, like Babylon.

HOOPOE
Lord love a duck . . . That would be some city.

PEISETAIROS
Once the city's been set up, Zeus should be asked to renounce his
claim of jurisdiction over it. If he says "No," a
holy war should be declared on him. The other
gods shouldn't be allowed to criss-cross your
territory with hard-ons like in the old days when

they came down after your Alcmenes and your
Alopes and your Semeles. If they do violate your
airspace, they should have seals stamped on their
cocks so they can't screw at will anymore.
Then an envoy should be sent to the humans to explain to them
that, in future, sacrifices should be made to the
birds first, then the gods. A bird should be paired
with each god, as would be deemed appropriate.
If a body's making a sacrifice to Aphrodite, for example, an
offering of wheat should be set before a
dickybird. In the case of a sheep being offered
to Poseidon, a little wheat should be dedicated
to a sea-going duck.
If it's a sacrifice to Heracles of the hearty appetite, plenty of big
honey-cakes should be laid before a gull.
If it's a ram to Zeus, king of the gods, then an offering should
be made to the raunchy little wren, the bird-
king, for whom a body should slay a sacrificial
gnat, one with its organs of procreation quite
uncompromised.

EUELPIDES
I like the gnat idea. "Now let great Zeus thunder . . ."   390

CHORUS LEADER
How will people know we're gods rather than common or garden
birds, jackdaws, or such? We'll still be wearing
our wings.

PEISETAIROS
Hermes is a god, isn't he? He wears wings. Others, too. Victory
has two golden wings. Eros, of course.
And Homer likens Iris to a frightened dove.

EUELPIDES
I'm worried that Zeus might send down one of his thunderbolts.
A *winged* one to boot.

PEISETAIROS

If humans, in their ignorance, don't give you your due and
worship the gods of Mount Olympus instead, all
you have to do is have a shower of sparrows fall
on their wheatfields and pick them clean. Then,
when they're starving to death, let's see their so-
called corn-goddess, Demeter, provide them with
wheat.

EUELPIDES

She'll have trouble explaining why she can't deliver on that one,
for sure.

PEISETAIROS

By way of further example, have the crows peck out the eyes of
their sheep and teams of oxen. Then let Apollo
the Apothecary prescribe a cure for them. I bet
he'll be charging an arm and a leg for that
prescription.

EUELPIDES

Tell those crows to lay off till I sell my pair of bullocks.

PEISETAIROS

If, however, they allow that you birds do indeed represent the
Supreme Deity, Life, Time, Poseidon—you name
it—then they'll reap the benefits.   400

CHORUS LEADER

Benefits? What benefits?

PEISETAIROS

To begin with, the locusts will not eat their vines, since a
company of owls and kestrels will rout them
entirely. Then, the weevils and wasps won't eat
the figs, since a troop of thrushes will wipe them
off the face of the earth.

CHORUS LEADER
How will we make them rich, though? That's their highest
priority.

PEISETAIROS
When they're looking for omens the birds can direct them to
the richest silver mines. They can predict the
outcome of any business venture. And no sea
captain will ever be lost again.

CHORUS LEADER
How will we ensure that?

PEISETAIROS
They'll always take their cue from a bird's flight pattern. "Don't
sail," one will say, "for the wind is strong." "Sail
now," says another, "and it'll be worth your
while."

EUELPIDES
I should buy a boat rather than stay with you.

PEISETAIROS
The birds will direct them to the treasure troves hidden away in
ancient times. You know where they are. You
know that expression, "A little bird told me . . ."?

EUELPIDES
I'll sell my boat, buy a spade, and dig up that buried treasure.

CHORUS LEADER
How can the birds bring men good health? That comes from the
gods, surely?

PEISETAIROS
A healthy bank balance adds up to the same thing.   410

EUELPIDES

If a man's not thriving financially he's not thriving full stop.

CHORUS LEADER

What about longevity? That also falls to the gods. Are men all
destined to die young?

PEISETAIROS

Not at all. The birds can extend their lives by at least three
hundred years.

CHORUS LEADER

Where will they come by those extra years?

PEISETAIROS

From their own allocations. The crow, for example, lives as long
as five men put together.

EUELPIDES

These bird-kings are going to be much better than Zeus.

PEISETAIROS

By a long shot. To begin with, we won't have to build temples
for them, with gold doors and all. They'll be
perfectly happy with the bushes and the sacred
oaks and the olive trees. We won't have to go to
Delphi or Ammon to make a sacrifice. We'll only
have to stand out among the arbutus and olive
trees with handfuls of corn, praying for a blessing
from the birds, and they'll bestow it on us
without further ado.

CHORUS LEADER

I can't believe we took you for our foe.
Now we'll follow you wherever you go.
Listening to your words,   420

we swear that if you stick with the birds
in their campaign against the gods,
you'll significantly shorten the odds
of their holding onto the special powers
that are rightfully ours.
We have the strength to do what we must do.
The finer points of strategy we'll leave to you.

HOOPOE

> By heavens. It's time to stop footering about. It's time to shake a
> leg and get a move on. First, though, why don't
> you come up and have a look around my nest?
> It's a somewhat unstately pile of twigs . . . I
> realize I didn't quite catch your names.

PEISETAIROS

> That's no problem. I'm Peisetairos.

EUELPIDES

> And I'm Euelpides. From Crio.   430

HOOPOE

> Step right up.

PEISETAIROS

> Thanks.

HOOPOE

> Make yourselves at home.

PEISETAIROS

> We'll be right with you.

HOOPOE

> That's it.

PEISETAIROS *(having trouble getting up the cliff-face)*
>   It occurs to me that . . . you know . . . how are we going to keep
>   up with you birds when you've got wings and we,
>   in a word, don't.

HOOPOE
>   You'll be just fine.

PEISETAIROS
>   I seem to remember something in Aesop about a fox who tried
>   to live with an eagle and how it didn't quite
>   work out.

HOOPOE
>   Don't bother your head worrying about that. There's a little root
>   you can nibble on that'll make you grow a wing
>   or two.

PEISETAIROS
>   Terrific.   440
(calls out to the slaves)
>   Xanthias . . . Manodorus . . . Bring up the bags.

CHORUS LEADER
>   Hi. Hoopoe.

HOOPOE
>   What's up?

CHORUS LEADER
>   Take these fellows with you and give them a good feed. But leave
>   us that sweet little nightingale. Send her out so
>   we can, you know, *play* with her.

PEISETAIROS
>   Oh do, do, do. Make that little birdy fly out of the reeds.

EUELPIDES
Yes, make her fly out. Let's have a look at that little nightingale.

HOOPOE
Well, if that's what you'd like . . .
(he calls out)
Procne, my dear, come out here and let the visitors see you.
(A curvaceous Procne emerges, carrying her flute.)

PEISETAIROS
What a beautiful, beautiful dollybird. All smooth and white.

EUELPIDES
You know what? I wouldn't mind throwing the leg over her.   450

PEISETAIROS
Look at the amount of gold on her. She's all got up like a
        bride-to-be.

EUELPIDES
I'd love to give her a good shagging.

PEISETAIROS
Get a load of her beak, you gomeril. It's so sharp you'd impale
        yourself on her.

EUELPIDES
That's no problem. It'd be no worse than eating an egg.
(Euelpides takes off Procne's mask.)
You have to contend with the hard bits before you get to the
        soft bits.
(The Hoopoe is dismayed by all this innuendo.)

HOOPOE
Let's go in.

PEISETAIROS
>   After you.
>   *(They climb up to the Hoopoe's house while the chorus sings the praises
>   of Procne.)*

CHORUS
>   Dearest one,
>   we love the dun   460
>   of your coat,
>   your reddish throat,
>   you who are first
>   flute of the forest.
>   Let your voice ring
>   out to Spring
>   that it may be heard
>   over the chorus of birds.
>   Come, you who live in the half-light
>   between night-going-on-day
>   or day-going-on-night,   470
>   you poor creatures of clay,
>   you poor specters, you poor shades
>   who fade and flitter between the portals
>   as leaves flitter and fade,
>   come listen to us, the immortals.
>   Let us, the ageless ones, those who don't perish,
>   tell it like it is
>   not only about our own peerage
>   but the sources of rivers, the seats of deities,
>   the origin of Chaos and the Dark   480
>   in which you're wont to dwell—
>   after which you may, for a lark,
>   advise that know-all, Prodicus, to go to hell.
>   For in times long gone by
>   there were only Chaos, Night, the Dark, and the pit
>   of Tartarus. No Earth. No Sky.
>   But black-winged Night would put

a wind-milted egg in the Dark's belly,
from which, in the way one thing
leads to another, Eros would sally   490
forth—Eros of the golden wings,
the bright and beautiful Eros
who would himself do the nasty
with Chaos in the pit of Tartarus,
so bringing our bird-dynasty
into being and leading the first of our line
to the light. There had been no ageless ones, you see,
until Eros would combine
those elements. Only then did Sky and Sea
and Earth exist as such.   500
Only then did the Blessed Ones exist.
So it is that we are much, much
older than the oldest of the Blessed.
That we're the seed and breed of Eros is clear
in many ways. Not only do we fly but
we're efficacious in love, as when some dear
beardless boy is persuaded to spread his butt
by the love-token of a goose or a purple gallinule
or a little red rooster.
All the best things come, as a rule,   510
from the birds. The very roster
of the seasons is decreed
by us. When the crane leaves these shores
for Libya it's time to put in the seed.
Then the sea captain can hang up his oar
and have a long lie in. Then Orestes can weave
himself a cloak so he doesn't get frostbite
as he relieves
travelers of theirs. The kite
lets us know it's time for the sheep to be shorn.   520
The swallow announces that light
summer clothes may be worn
with impunity. We're like the oracles at Ammon

and Dodona and Delphi and Phoebus Apollo
rolled into one. That's why it's so common
for you to consult the birds as to which way to go
in both business affairs and affairs of the heart.
That little bird tells you which way to jump.
The slang term "bird" may also import and impart
the sense of a casual remark, a sneeze, a chance encounter,
          a thump,   530
a class of a flunkey
or, in at least one figure,
an ass or Egyptian donkey.
Our role as augurs keeps on getting bigger and bigger.

CHORUS LEADER

Take us for your gods
and we'll say our sooth
on fair winds, cold snaps, the sudden turn
from the mildly to the stiflingly hot.

Take us for your gods
and we won't be aloof.   540
We won't be in the least standoffish. We won't spurn
you like Zeus from some remote spot.

Take us for your gods
and we'll promise that health, wealth, youth,
laughter, dancing, parties, and everything else for which you
                     might yearn
will be your, and your ancestors', lot.

CHORUS

Muse of the thornbush
tiotiotiotiotinx
blessed with so many notes,
with whom, from a leafy ash,   550
tiotiotiotiotinx

across the mountains and plains
I would release from my throat
for Pan or Cybele the strains
totototototototototinx
of some hymn, a hymn on whose melody
Phrynikhos would feed like a honey-bee.
How would you like to come and live with the birds?
You may rest assured
that our laws are somewhat different from your own.   560
Here it's illegal for a son
to hit his father. With us, a strapping young lad
thinks nothing of going a few rounds with his dad
in the cockpit. Where one of you is branded
as a runaway slave, we see a francolin, speckled and banded.
If you happen to be a Phrygian slave, like Spintharos,
you're a frigg-it-bird. Whereas,
if you're like Exekestides, a Carian crow,
you can always find a way to grow
some grand*feathers*. And if that Lundy, Peisias,   570
wants to open the gates and let our enemies pass
through unimpeded, how could he fail
to be a partridge, like his father, famous for turning tail?
So the swans would sing
tiotiotiotiotinx
to Apollo, beating time with their wings,
tiotiotiotiotinx
on the Hebros banks
to the airy clouds   580
tiotiotiotiotinx
till the beasts in their ranks
all cowered and were cowed
and the ocean waves would suddenly relent
totototototototinx
as the gods of Olympus and a throng
of Muses and Graces all sent
up their joyful answering song

tiotiotiotiotinx.
There's nothing handier than having the wings of a bird.
Suppose, for example, you get bored   590
with one of these tragic plays. You could fly
off home, have a bite of lunch, and return in the sweet by and by.
And if Patrokleides there happens to be taken short
he needn't stain his drawers. He need only let a fart,
float off, do his business, and float back inside.
What if you're getting a bit on the side
with your neighbor's wife? Once you see him in the reserved
                    section,
you can fly to her house, give her a meat injection,
and be back again. If you're wise,
you'll see there's nothing handier   600
than a pair of wings. You've seen the spectacular rise
of Dieitrephes, who, on the strength of a couple of wicker bottle-
                    flaps,
went from captain to colonel to commander—
a shit-hot, shit-kicking satrap.
(Peisetairos and Euelpides enter, each wearing a set of wings.)

PEISETAIROS
    Get a load of this.

EUELPIDES
    I've never seen anything more hilarious.

PEISETAIROS
    What's so funny?

EUELPIDES
    Your wings, you glipe. You know what you remind me of?

PEISETAIROS
    I know what *you* look like. A half-finished painting of a goose.

EUELPIDES
You look like a blackbird with a bowl-haircut. 610

PEISETAIROS
We'd better stop turning on ourselves or we'll be like the eagle in
Aeschylus, shot down by an arrow fletched with
an eagle's feather.

CHORUS
Come on, what's next on the agenda?

PEISETAIROS
First of all we need a name for our new city state. Something
with a bit of a ring to it. Then we'll have to make
a sacrifice to the gods.

EUELPIDES
That sounds about right.

CHORUS
So what name are you thinking of?

PEISETAIROS
What about using that good old Lacedaimonian name—Sparta?

EUELPIDES
Sparta-farta. I wouldn't stoop to using spartum-rope for my
spare bed, never mind anything else.

PEISETAIROS *(steadying himself for the pun he's about to make)*
That's because you have enough *suppart* as it is.

CHORUS
Seriously. What's the name to be?

EUELPIDES

We want something appropriate to a place coming down with
birds. Something to do with the clouds and the
sky. Something . . . full of air.   620

PEISETAIROS

It's coming to me . . . Cucucumulopolis . . . No . . .
Nimborough . . . No . . . Ballybirdeen . . . No . . .
Cuckwick . . . No . . . Cirrocester . . . No . . .
Gowkstead . . . No . . . I've got it . . .
Nebulbulfast.

CHORUS

That's it. That's a fine big lump of a name.

EUELPIDES

Nebulbulfast? Isn't that where those blowhards, Theogenes and
Aischines, keep their offshore accounts?

PEISETAIROS

More to the point, it's above the plain of Phlegra, where the gods
beat the giants in the finals of the World Boasting
Association.

CHORUS

What a terrific city. What a toddling town.
But which god will keep it safe and sound?
Whose statue will we deck out with a ceremonial gown?

PEISETAIROS

What about Athena herself?

EUELPIDES

You don't seriously think a city is in good shape when some god-
turned-woman is standing guard there, armed to
the teeth, while the likes of Kleisthenes ponces
about at his loom?

CHORUS
> Seeing the times that are in it,   630
> we need someone to guard the paleibisades,
> we need someone to patrol the city linnets.

PEISETAIROS
> Shouldn't that be one of you? One of those Persian high-fliers,
> > maybe?

CHORUS
> The very thing. A Persian cock
> should be well-prepared for midnight raids,
> should feel quite at home on a rock.

PEISETAIROS *(to Euelpides)*
> Why don't you get on up there and give the wall-builders a hand?
> > Why don't you bring them some rubble? Why
> > don't you roll up your sleeves and mix a load of
> > mortar? Why don't you carry a hod, fall off the
> > ladder, post a few sentries, keep the fire smoored,
> > run around with a bell to keep everyone on their
> > toes, spend a night on the job, send out a couple
> > of emissaries—one to the gods, one to the
> > humans—and generally get a move on?

EUELPIDES
> And why don't you take a flying fuck? Why should I always be
> > the one busting a gut?

PEISETAIROS
> Shake a leg. You know that if you're not around
> to keep an eye on these clowns,   640
> Nebulbulfast will never get off the ground.
> *(Euelpides takes off vertically, with a farewell flap, by means of an*
> > *elaborate hoist.)*

I myself had better try to get hold of a priest to lead the
                    procession for the ritual sacrifice to these
                    new gods.
(to Xanthias)
Boy. You take the basket and the holy water.
(Peisetairos exits as Xanthias and Manes set up a rudimentary altar.)

CHORUS
Indeed I am, indeed I am
moved to make an offering
to these new gods not only of the usual things
but also a little bit of a goat or lamb.

CHORUS LEADER
Let the dreaded Chairis pipe along
by way of accompaniment to Apollo's song.
*(A raven-masked Chairis enters playing his pipe, very poorly, while
                    Peisetairos returns with the priest, carrying what
                    look like some spare parts for a goat.)*

PEISETAIROS
Hey, you. Stop your huffing and puffing.   650
(Exit Chairis.)
I've seen many wild and wonderful things, I can tell you, but
                    never a crow that blows.
(he hands the "goat" to the priest)
Now, priest, it's time for you to make a sacrifice to the new gods.

PRIEST
That I will, as soon as I have the basket-man in tow.
(The priest, Peisetairos, Xanthias, and Manes process around the altar.)
Let us pray to the bird of the hearth, to the kite who oversees
                    the altar, to the male and female gods of
                    Olympus . . .

PEISETAIROS
To Poseidon, the stork of Sounion, let us pray.

PRIEST

To the swan of Pythia, the swan of Delos, to the corncrake, Leto,
to the thistle-finch, Artemis . . .

PEISETAIROS

To the sacred finch of Notaninch . . .

PRIEST

To Sabazios, the sparrow, and the ostrich, that mother of all
sparrows . . .

PEISETAIROS

The mother of Cleocritus, you mean, sprachaling along like a
wheelbarrow.

PRIEST

May they shower blessings upon the citizens of Nebulbulfast and
their allies in Chios.   660

PEISETAIROS

Oh, sure. Let's never forget that special relationship with the
Chians.

PRIEST

To the Purple Gallinule, the Pelican, the Shag, the Spotted
Eagle, the famous Capercaillie, the Peacock,
the Warbler, the Teal, the Skua, the Heron,
the Gannet, the Marsh Tit, the Titmouse . . .

PEISETAIROS

Hold on a minute . . . How come you're calling down all
these ospreys and vultures? Take a look at the
"sacrificial victim." A single kite could carry it
off without any bother to it. I think it's about
time you gathered up your garlands and moved
right along. I'll do the honors. I'll officiate
myself.

(Peisetairos sends the priest packing.)

CHORUS

>As the priest his hands asperges
>once more our holy song surges
>to one of the heaven-born—
>for one and one alone might
>satisfy his appetite
>on this beard and these horns.

PEISETAIROS *(raising a knife over the "sacrifice")*

>Let us make a holy offering to the gods with wings.   670

(A wandering, half-naked bard enters.)

BARD

>O let me entreat the Muse
>to help a bare bard broadcast
>this news that will stay news—
>the founding of Nebulbulfast.

PEISETAIROS

>What's up? Who the hell are you?

BARD

>I am a bard of high degree
>and honeyed words
>and strict measures, oh see,
>though they're strictly for the birds.
>I am, if I may use   680
>a phrase from Homer, "a bondsman of the Muse."

PEISETAIROS

>A bondsman? How come you've got such long hair if you're a
>   bondsman?

BARD

>No. That's not what I mean. Every poet is a "wholehearted
>   bondsman of the Muse." It's a phrase from
>   Homer.

PEISETAIROS

> Wholehearted? No wonder you've so many *holes* in your vest.
> > What brings you mooching round here?

BARD

> Well, I've already composed quite a few songs in praise of
> > Nebulbulfast. Some excellent round songs . . .
> > Some songs for female chorus . . . Some songs
> > in the style of Simonides . . .

PEISETAIROS

> When did you compose these songs? When did you start?

BARD

> I've been singing the praises of this city for a long time now.

PEISETAIROS

> How is it I'm only now celebrating its coming into being? How is
> > it I'm naming it as we speak?

BARD

> That's because the Muse wastes no time
> and comes up with a rhyme   690
> in the twinkling of a horse's hoof.
> But you, holy Hieron, forsooth,
> whose name, according to Pindar,
> is a play on the "holy" altar and its "holy" cinders,
> you who are one of the founding fathers
> of Athens, may it please you to give me whatever
> it pleases you to see
> fit to please give to poor me.

PEISETAIROS

> This guy's really bad news. We'll have to give him something to
> > get shot of him.

(to Xanthias)

You, you've got a jacket and a shirt both. Take off the jacket and
　　　　　give it to our esteemed bard.　　　　　　　　　　700
(to the bard)
　Here, take this. It seems it's not only your verses that are frigid.

BARD

　The Muse happily accepts this gift
　though once again a poem by Pindar I will lift.

PEISETAIROS

　How will we ever get this guy to shift?

BARD

　Among the Sycthian nomads
　there wanders one poor soul
　who's feeling very, very sad
　for want of a shirt of wool . . .
　You get my drift?

PEISETAIROS

　I get your drift.　　　　　　　　　　　　　　　　　　710
(to Xanthias)
　Give him the shirt. We have to help a poet.
(to the bard)
　Take this and make yourself scarce. Pronto.

BARD

　I will shortly be a thing of the past
　but I will compose, in honor of Nebulbulfast,
　poems such as this:
　Hail to the city of the golden thrones
　and freezing rain.
　I know in my bones
　I have come to the city of the snowy plains.

PEISETAIROS

You can put all that codology behind you now that you've got
a coat.   720

(The bard exits.)

That was a spot of bother I hadn't anticipated. How on earth did
he know about Nebulbulfast so early on?

(to Xanthias)

You. Take the holy water. We'll go round again. And let's try to
have a little peace and quiet.

(An oracle monger enters with a bundle of oracles.)

ORACLE MONGER

Hold on. Don't start the sacrifice just yet.

PEISETAIROS

And who would you be?

ORACLE MONGER

An oracle monger.

PEISETAIROS

No way. Out you get.

ORACLE MONGER

Don't make light of the powers of divination. You should be
aware, for example, of one of Bakis' oracles
referring quite specifically to Nebulbulfast.

PEISETAIROS

How is it, then, that you yourself had no intimation of the
founding of this city?

ORACLE MONGER

The divine voice must have jammed the signal in some way.

PEISETAIROS
Okay. Let's hear what Bakis had to say.   730

ORACLE MONGER
"Where you wolves and crows together find
there will be a city of the mind,
as in that impossible zone
between Corinth and Sicyon."

PEISETAIROS
What do those shithead Corinthians have to do with me?

ORACLE MONGER
What Bakis meant, in his riddling way, was a city in the air.
(continues to quote)
"First offer to Pandora a white ram or goat.
Then give the first to come along and quote
this oracle a pair of sandals and a new coat."

PEISETAIROS
Sandals? It mentions sandals?   740

ORACLE MONGER
You want to check it?
(quotes again)
"Give him a cup of wine and a pile of roasted guts."

PEISETAIROS
It mentions guts, too?

ORACLE MONGER
Have a look yourself.
(quotes again)
"For if you do as I implore
you will like an eagle soar.
If you give me the bum's rush
you won't even get to be a woodpecker, dove or a lousy thrush."

PEISETAIROS
    All that's there in your book?

ORACLE MONGER
    I promise you. Why don't you have a look?   750

PEISETAIROS
    That's funny. Because your oracle's not at all like the one I have.
    (He reaches into his coat and takes out a padded phallus, which he
                          examines.)
    I wrote this out myself at Apollo's behest:
    "Should there come a stranger to your hut
    most desirous of the sacrificial guts
    it behooves you to kick him in the nuts."

ORACLE MONGER
    You're kidding me.

PEISETAIROS
    Here . . .
(offering him the phallus)
    Why don't you take a look?
    Do not spare him even if it is
    an eagle or Lampon or the great Diopethes.   760

ORACLE MONGER
    All that's there in your book?

PEISETAIROS *(again offering him the phallus)*
    As I say, why don't you have a look? Now, move along, for the
                  good of your health.

ORACLE MONGER
    Poor me. Poor, poor pitiful me.

PEISETAIROS
>Run along and oracle-monger somewhere else.
>*(As the oracle monger exits, the famous geometer and astronomer Meton*
>>*enters, wearing a pair of high-heeled women's*
>>*shoes. He carries surveyor's poles.)*

METON *(gravely)*
>I come to you . . .

PEISETAIROS
>Another smartass. So what's your bag? What's your game-plan?
>*(taking in the high heels)*
>And what's with the fuck-me pumps?

METON
>I propose to geometrize the sky and parcel it out in subdivisions.

PEISETAIROS
>Who do you think you are, old man? Gerry Mander?

METON
>Not at all. I'm Meton. The one and only. A household name
>>throughout Greece, as well as in Colonus.   770

PEISETAIROS
>Of course. Your hydraulic cock.

METON *(hurt)*
>Clock.

PEISETAIROS
>What's all that stuff you've brought?

METON
>Air-survey-sticks. You must understand that the air takes the
>>form of . . . resembles nothing so much as a grill-

hood . . . So that, by applying the ruler from
above—see?—this curved one, and inserting
the compass—with me so far?

PEISETAIROS
Frankly, no . . .

METON
Then, by applying the straight ruler, so that the circle becomes
squared, with the marketplace at the very center,
you have the streets leading away from it in
straight lines . . . It's like how a star, which is
round, of course, sends out perfectly straight
beams of light.

PEISETAIROS
Heavens above. The man's a veritable Thales. But . . . Meton . . .

METON
Yes?

PEISETAIROS
Speaking to you as a friend, let me give you a word of advice. I
think you'd better leave while you still can.

METON
Why so? What's the problem?   780

PEISETAIROS
The people here are like the people in Sparta. Complete strangers
being given twenty-four hours to get out.
Punishment beatings.

METON
What? There's still civil unrest? They're still divided along party
lines?

PEISETAIROS
  No. Far from it.

METON
  What, then?

PEISETAIROS
  They're absolutely in agreement on one thing.

METON
  Yes?

PEISETAIROS
  They don't like dopes. Fuck the Dope. No Dope Here.

METON
  I'll be off, then.

PEISETAIROS
  I'm not sure you're going to make it in time . . . Those
                punishment beatings are getting closer,
                I fear . . . Yes, I do believe . . .
(attacks Meton with his padded phallus)

METON
  Uh oh. I think I'm in deep shit.   790

PEISETAIROS
  Didn't I tell you? Now . . . Why don't you just take a few of those
                measured steps of yours back to wherever you
                came from?
*(Meton exits and an Ombirdsman enters. He is dressed in Persian-style
                clothes and carries two ballot boxes, one marked
                Yes, the other No.)*

OMBIRDSMAN
Where are those people from the consulate?

PEISETAIROS
Now what? King Ashurbanipal?

OMBIRDSMAN
I've come here as an Ombirdsman, an independent observer
appointed by the High Commissioner of the
UN, the United Nebulbulfasts.

PEISETAIROS
An Ombirdsman? Who sent you?

OMBIRDSMAN *(showing his accreditation)*
The High Commissioner. Teleas.

PEISETAIROS
I see. So you'll be wanting to get your cut now and then clear off,
right?

OMBIRDSMAN
Well, sort of. I need to get back to the assembly to oversee a little
item of business I arranged with Pharnakes.

PEISETAIROS
Great. So why don't I just give you your cut now? All set?
(whacks the Ombirdsman with the phallus)

OMBIRDSMAN
Hey. What's that for? What's that all about?   800

PEISETAIROS
That's all about the punch-up in the assembly that featured your
friend Pharnakes.

OMBIRDSMAN
> Look everybody . . . Look . . . I'm an Ombirdsman and I'm being
> > assaulted.

PEISETAIROS
> Fuck off. And take your ballot boxes with you.
> *(to the audience)*
> > Can you believe this? We haven't even dedicated the city
> > > and they're already sending independent
> > > observers . . .
> *(The Ombirdsman exits. A statute seller enters, reading from a scroll.)*

STATUTE SELLER
> "If, however, a citizen of Nebulbulfast should commit an offense
> > against a citizen of Athens . . ."

PEISETAIROS
> More legislation.

STATUTE SELLER
> I am a statute seller, and I come to promulgate new laws and
> > orders.

PEISETAIROS
> What sort of laws?

STATUTE SELLER
> That the Nebulbulfastians use the same weights and measures
> > and currency as the Olophuxians.

PEISETAIROS
> You mean the same as the Allafuckians. The same as the people
> > of Ballymoaney?   810
> *(raises the phallus threateningly)*

STATUTE SELLER
What's wrong? What's your problem?

PEISETAIROS
Take your law and order and move it right along or bitter indeed
shall be the law and order I mete out unto you.
*(Peisetairos beats the statute seller about the head as the Ombirdsman
reappears.)*

OMBIRDSMAN
I hereby summon Peisetairos to appear at the April assizes on a
charge of assault and battery.

PEISETAIROS
You don't say? You still here?

STATUTE SELLER
"Whereas if anyone should fail to receive the Ombirdsman with
the appropriate . . ."

PEISETAIROS
I don't believe it. You're still here too?

OMBIRDSMAN
I'll see you hauled over the coals. You'll pay the maximum
penalty. Ten thousand drachmas.

PEISETAIROS
Is that a fact? Then let me put paid to your ballot boxes.
(A minor scuffle ensues.)

STATUTE SELLER *(menacingly)*
You remember the night you took a crap at the foot of the sacred
column where the statutes are handed down? I
may have to bring that into evidence.

PEISETAIROS

    Hey. Grab that guy.   820

(The statute seller flees.)

    Hey. Why don't you stick around?

(to Manes and Xanthias)

    Okay. Let's try to get inside as fast as we can and finish off the
             sacrificial rites.

*(They gather up all their belongings, including the "goat," and go into
the cliff-face.)*

CHORUS

    Now to us, the Blessed Ones, to whom all is known,
    will the humans offer
    their sacrifice on a bloody stone.
    Now it is us, the birds, who will watch over
    their fields of crops
    and destroy all weevils and worms
    and generally put a stop
    to those who trade and traffic in evil and harm.   830
    For we'll act as wardens
    and put to flight
    from their sweet-smelling gardens
    anything that creeps and bites.

CHORUS LEADER

    Speaking of creeps, it's time we put a price on the head
    of Diagoras of Melos, time also to offer a reward
    of one talent for any tyrant, living or dead.
    Another talent to him who nails Philokrates to a board,
    four talents to anyone bringing
    him in alive. This is the self-same Philokrates who shows   840
    only a talent for stringing
    up siskins and selling them at seven an obol, the Philokrates
             who blows
    up a thrush to help improve its image,
    who shoves up a blackbird's neb a bit

of its own plumage,
who keeps a rock dove in a cage by way of a decoy or bait.
For this is the decree we're issuing today.
Anyone keeping a bird prisoner must ensure
its immediate release. If you don't obey,   850
you will be caught by us and used,
in your turn, as a lure.

CHORUS
    Happy the birds who need
    no winter kirtle
    to keep them warm
    nor are overcome
    in the middle of June
    by sudden heat waves
    but live in shady meads
    where the cricket hymns and hums
    at high noon   860
    and winter in caves
    while in spring we feed
    on white myrtle
    and fresh herbs from the herb-farm.

CHORUS
    To the adjudicators we wish to say
    that, should you settle on this play,
    more good things will come your way
    than came to Paris ever.
    In the first place, you'll have no end
    of owls, the ones you can spend,   870
    the ones that legally tend,
    the ones stamped on pieces of silver.
    Should you judge us the best,
    long will those owls nest
    in your wallets, leaving a little interest,
    once again tender and legal.

Your houses will look as though they were meant
to be temples rather than tenements
what with their triangular spread-wing impediments
known as "eagles."   880
And when you go out for some chow
you'll be fit to eat a cow
since you'll all be endowed
with our "ravenous" appetites.
But should you somehow fail to choose
us as number one, you'll be the ones to lose.
Just for that
you'll need to wear a statue's metal "hat"
for when we do our number twos
we'll cover you completely with birdshite.   890
(Peisetairos reemerges from the cliff-face.)

PEISETAIROS
>The ritual sacrifice has gone like a dream. But why hasn't anyone
>come back from the wall to report on how things
>are going? Hold on . . . Here comes a runner.

(The first runner enters.)

FIRST RUNNER
>Where . . . Where is he? Where . . . Where is he? Where . . .
>Where is he? Where is Peisetairos the leader?

PEISETAIROS
>Over here.

FIRST RUNNER
>It's finished. The wall's finished.

PEISETAIROS
>That's terrific news.

FIRST RUNNER

It's an amazing job. The top of the wall's so wide that Proxenides
and Theogenes, the blowhard, could drive their
chariots past each other even if their horses were
as big as the wooden horse of Troy.

PEISETAIROS

Heavens above.

FIRST RUNNER

What's more, it's a hundred fathoms high. I measured it myself.

PEISETAIROS

You're kidding. How did it get to be so tall?

FIRST RUNNER

It was built by the birds and the birds alone. There were none of
your Egyptian brickmakers, stoneworkers, or
carpenters involved. The birds did it all with
their own hands. It was amazing to watch. Thirty
thousand cranes came from Libya, all of them
loaded with ballast. The corncrakes chipped away
at the stones with their beaks. Ten thousand
storks were making bricks. The water was carried
up by lapwings and other river birds.   900

PEISETAIROS

Who did the plastering?

FIRST RUNNER

The herons, carrying hods.

PEISETAIROS

How did they get the mortar into the hods?

FIRST RUNNER

That was done by the geese. They shoveled it in with their feet.

PEISETAIROS

No mean feet.

FIRST RUNNER

You should have seen the ducks laying bricks, wearing their
mason's aprons. Then there were the swallows,
with their trowels full of mud.

PEISETAIROS

There'll be no need to hire laborers after this. But tell me . . .
What about the wooden parts of the wall? Who
looked after that?

FIRST RUNNER

There were bird carpenters as well. Woodpeckers, of course, who
roughed out the gates with their beaks. They
made so much noise the place sounded like a
shipyard. Now the gates are all in place, sentries
have been posted and watch fires lit . . . I think
I'll go and get myself cleaned up while you deal
with all the other stuff.

(First runner exits.)

CHORUS LEADER

What's your problem now? Why do you look aghast?
Can you believe how quickly they've built Nebulbulfast?   910

PEISETAIROS

I scarcely can believe it. It sounds like a tall tale. What's next? If
it isn't another runner. It looks as if he's on the
warpath.

(A terrified second runner rushes in.)

SECOND RUNNER
> Wawawawawawawawawawa.

PEISETAIROS
> What's up? What's the problem?

SECOND RUNNER
> We've had a terrible setback. A terrible breach of security. One of
> the gods, one of Zeus' outfit, has just entered our
> air space. He flew right past our jackdaws.

PEISETAIROS
> Things really are out of control. Which god is it?

SECOND RUNNER
> We weren't able to identify him. He did have wings. That's all
> we know.

PEISETAIROS
> Why weren't the border patrol dispatched immediately?

SECOND RUNNER
> They were dispatched. We've sent out thirty thousand mounted
> bow-and-arrowhawks. Everything with hooked
> talons has been mobilized—kestrels, buzzards,
> vultures, eagle-owls, the eagles themselves—the
> air is full of the whoosh and whir of their wings
> as they go about hunting down the god. He can't
> be far away. What's that? It sounds as if he might
> be just overhead.

*(Second runner rushes off, terrified, to a sound not unlike that of a
helicopter about to touch down.)*

PEISETAIROS
> Break out the slings and bows. This way . . . This way . . . Fire at
> will . . . Somebody put a sling in my hand.

CHORUS

War has broken out. Unspeakable war   920
between the gods and the birds.
Keep a sharp lookout since, in mid-air,
some whirligigging god is heard.
(Rainbow enters by means of the stage hoist. Her voluminous gown
billows like a sail.)

PEISETAIROS

Hey. You there. Where do you think you're going? Stop right
there. Stop it now. Who are you? Where are
you from?

RAINBOW

From the gods I do come, from the Olympians.

PEISETAIROS

And your name? Would you be the good ship Paralos or the good
ship Salaminia?

RAINBOW

I'm Rainbow, the fast cruiser.

PEISETAIROS

The fast cruiser?
(eyes her up and down)
Sounds about right.

RAINBOW

What's going on here?

PEISETAIROS

Why doesn't a buzzard get up there and put her under arrest?   930

RAINBOW

Under arrest? That's a positively dreadful idea.

PEISETAIROS
I'd love to get my fingers in your pot of gold, Miss Rainbow.

RAINBOW
This is all so positively dreadful.

PEISETAIROS
Well, my little fast cruiser, by which gate did you violate our air
space?

RAINBOW
Gate? Violate?

PEISETAIROS
Get a load of her. She pretends to be so dumb. Maybe you got
too "close" to the jackdaws? Not saying? Did you
take some little storkie "under your wing"?

RAINBOW
Who is this personage?

PEISETAIROS
Did you or didn't you?

RAINBOW
Have you lost your mind entirely?

PEISETAIROS
Have you taken the right "route"? Have you gone through all
the proper "channels" as far as the birds are
concerned?   940

RAINBOW
You're a positive fool. I've had nothing to do with channels,
proper or otherwise.

PEISETAIROS

So how come you're flying so low, Miss Rainbow, through our
air space?

RAINBOW

I didn't know of any other route.

PEISETAIROS

Well, this route's no longer open. You're in a seriously
compromised position here. Don't you know
that you could be arrested, Miss Rainbow or
no Miss Rainbow, and put to death?

RAINBOW

Death? But I'm positively a Deathless One.

PEISETAIROS

We'll put you to death anyhow. You must understand that we
can't possibly allow a situation to develop where
we're supposedly in command while you gods
carry on as if nothing has happened, as if it's a
free for all. You've got to get your ass in gear. You
have to recognize the pecking order.

(conspiratorially)

So. You can tell me. What brought you flying down here with
those magnificent twin engines?

RAINBOW

I'm on a mission to earth. I was sent by Zeus, my father, to
instruct you mortals to offer ritual sacrifices to
the gods. You must slaughter sheep on the sacred
hearths and fill the streets with the smell of
burning fat.

PEISETAIROS

I'm missing something. Which gods are you talking about?

RAINBOW
>*Which* gods? Us. The gods in heaven. *The* gods.   950

PEISETAIROS
>*You're* gods?

RAINBOW
>Are there others I should know about?

PEISETAIROS
>The only gods to whom mortals now offer sacrifices are not,
>>heavens above, the gods above in heaven but
>>the birds.

RAINBOW
>Oh, foolish man. Oh, foolish, foolish man. Don't turn against the
>>gods lest they turn against you, lest Justice herself
>>take Zeus' axe to you, lest you and everything
>>you own be burned to a cinder by a stray
>>lightning bolt.

PEISETAIROS
>Hey, Miss Rainbow. Miss Rainbow Warrior. Let's have less of
>>the big talk. Who are you trying to scare? Some
>>Lydian, maybe, or some frigging Phrygian? You
>>ought to know that if Zeus keeps giving me grief,
>>I'll send fire-bearing eagles to blanket-bomb his
>>palace.
>You remember how he once found that one Old Coot,
>>Porphyrion, almost too much for him? If he
>>doesn't watch out, I'll send a squadron of six
>>hundred Old Coots, in leopard skins to boot,
>>to launch an air attack against him.
>As for you, Miss Rainbow Warrior, Miss Dreamboat, if you give
>>me any more bother, I promise I'll ram and
>>board you. And you might be pleasantly

surprised by my prowess, despite my advanced
years, my prowess with the old triple-prow.

RAINBOW
Be off with you, you positive little horror.

PEISETAIROS
Be off with you, yourself.

RAINBOW
You mark my words. When my father gets wind of this episode,
he'll deal with you appropriately.   960
(Rainbow is whisked away by the stage hoist.)

PEISETAIROS
That's it. Take yourself off. Go find yourself a younger man,
someone with a bit less fire in his belly.

CHORUS
The gods of Olympus are at last
barred from the city of Nebulbulfast.
Never again will smoke rise
from our altars to their skies.

PEISETAIROS
What on earth's happened to that runner I sent down below?
Isn't he ever coming back?
(A third runner rushes in.)

THIRD RUNNER
Hail, Peisetairos. O blessed one. O wisest of all wise guys. O most
famous one. Your lordship. Your excellency. Your
eminence . . . Aren't you ever going to say
anything?

PEISETAIROS
What's that?

THIRD RUNNER

    I wish to present you, as a token of the esteem in which you are
        held by the international community, with this
        golden crown.

PEISETAIROS

    I accept . . . I accept . . . But why would the international
        community want to honor me?   970

THIRD RUNNER

    Simple. Because you've set up such a famous city in the air. Its
        fame has now spread far and wide. For before
        you laid out Nebulbulfast, everybody was
        preoccupied with the Spartans. It was Sparta
        this, Sparta that. Everybody wore their hair long,
        Sparta style. They fasted, Sparta style. They never
        took a bath, in the great Socratic tradition. They
        even carried Spartan shillelaghs.
  Now everything's changed. Now everybody's preoccupied with
        birds. Now it's bird this, bird that. They walk like
        birds. They talk like birds. They're no sooner out
        of bed in the morning than they've lit out for the
        sky-court for a little nit-picking. Then they flock
        to the law book-shops, where they browse
        through the papyrus scrolls of the latest decrees
        and ordinances.
  They're so taken with this bird thing that they've even taken bird
        nicknames. One of them's called "Partridge"
        because of the way he hirples along. The horse
        breeder, Menippus, has been branded "Swallow."
        Opountios is known as "the Raven with One
        Eye," Philocles as "Lark," Theogenes as
        "Shelldrake," Lykourgos as "Ibis," Chairephon
        as "Nighthawk," and Syracosius as "Popinjay."
        Meidias they call "Quail," because of that stupid
        look on his face, like the look on a quail that's

just been hit over the head in a quail-flipping
contest.
The bird thing has got into their songs as well. They're all singing
about swallows and little ducks and goosey-
goosey ganders and turtledoves. If they're not
borne on the wings of love, it's at least a feather.
That's the way things have gone down below.
And I'll tell you something else for nothing. There'll be
thousands of them making their way up here
looking for wings and claw extensions, so you'd
better make sure you've plenty in stock.

PEISETAIROS
Well then, we'd better get a move on.
(to Xanthias and Manes)
Hurry up, there. Fill every bucket and basket you can find with
wings and bring them out when they're ready. I'll
stay here and greet the customers.

CHORUS
It looks as if the population's about to swell . . .

PEISETAIROS
Let's hope for a little luck as well.

CHORUS
Our hopes are now higher than anything . . .   980

PEISETAIROS
Hurry up, Manes, with that bucket of wings.

CHORUS
We can think of no finer way to spend our days
than where Wisdom, Grace, and Love hold sway.

PEISETAIROS
Hurry up, Manes . . . We haven't got all day.

CHORUS
    Let wings be piled high on the trays
    that we may beat . . .

PEISETAIROS
                this fellow like a dray.

CHORUS
    He's a "beast of burden," as they say.

PEISETAIROS
    Hurry up, Manodorus, or you'll get no hay.

CHORUS
    And, Peisetairos, you must yourself
    hurry up and lay out the wings on the shelf   990
    according to how a mortal might kit
    himself out—be it a poet's "wings of song,"
    a commander's "naval wing," a soothsayer's "wing
    and a prayer"—
    so that each may easily find his proper fit.

PEISETAIROS *(to Manes)*
    Suffering ducks! If you don't stir your stumps
    I'll give you one almighty fucking thump.
(Peisetairos runs after Manes, threatening to beat him up. A birdnik
               enters, singing in a high nasal twang.)

BIRDNIK
    I want to fly
    on an eagle's wing.
    I want to get high   1000
    more than anything.
    I want to roam
    over the bitter, blue-gray foam.

PEISETAIROS
>   That third runner was absolutely right. Here comes a young
>   fellow looking for "an eagle's wing."

BIRDNIK
>   The flying. There's nothing like it. It's totally the vibe.

PEISETAIROS
>   I'm missing something here.

BIRDNIK
>   I'm a birdnik. You know? I want to hang out with you guys. Live
>   by your moral code.

PEISETAIROS
>   Moral code? What aspect of our moral code?

BIRDNIK
>   The whole package. Particularly that stuff about it being okay to
>   strangle and stab your father.

PEISETAIROS
>   It's true. We do think it's character-building, in a certain sense,
>   for a young fellow to get stuck into his old man.   1010

BIRDNIK
>   That's why I want to come up here. I want to do in my da and
>   collect his nest-egg.

PEISETAIROS
>   The only trouble is that the birds have another law, set down in
>   the ancient edicts known as *The Heronhests*, to
>   wit: "Insofar as a Stork-father doth support a
>   Stork-son, it behooves the son to support the
>   father."

BIRDNIK

> A fat lot of good it did me to come here. To be told that I'm
> > obliged to look after the old man.

PEISETAIROS

> On the contrary. If you've come here with an open mind, I can
> > fix you up like a real War Orphan. First of all, let
> > me give you a bit of advice, something I learned
> > for myself when I was your age. In a word or two,
> > don't hit your father.

(Peisetairos hands the birdnik a crest and a spur.)

> Now, if you take this white cockade in one hand and this spur in
> > the other . . .

(sets a helmet on his head)

> Imagine you've got a rooster's crest on the top of your head . . .
> > There you are . . . You're all set to do guard duty,
> > go on maneuvers, earn your own keep, and
> > generally lay off your father . . . If you feel like
> > kicking some ass, take yourself over to the
> > Thracian front and give *them* what for.

BIRDNIK

> You know . . . What you say makes a lot of sense . . . a lot of
> > sense. I'm going to do exactly as you say.

PEISETAIROS

> Then sense is exactly what you have, my boy.

(The birdnik exits. Kinesias, a poet, enters singing.)

KINESIAS

> I've reached the heights
> of Olympus on wings that are light   1020
> as well as being fragile
> and exceedingly agile . . .

PEISETAIROS
>This character needs a truckload of wings to make him
>>lighten up.

KINESIAS
>With a fearless mind and body I rode
>along that long and winding . . .

PEISETAIROS
>It's got to be Kinesias, barest of bards. Why have you come
>>hobbling along here?

KINESIAS *(begins by speaking, ends by singing the line)*
>I want to sing like a bird,
>loud and clear as a nightingale . . .

PEISETAIROS
>Please stop singing and just *say* what you want.

KINESIAS
>I want a pair of wings so that I can fly up into the nebulous
>>reaches and find some snow-capped, airy airs.   1030

PEISETAIROS
>You expect to pluck airs out of the air?

KINESIAS
>Of course. That's where poetry comes from. At its best, poetry
>>is airy, at once dark and shot through with light,
>>moving in every sense. Let me give you an
>>example.

PEISETAIROS
>No. Please. Don't do that.

KINESIAS

But I must. Let me run through the whole thing for you.
(begins to sing)

The very clouds, with their golden flecks,
are like birds with big, long necks . . .

PEISETAIROS

Hold on . . .

KINESIAS

Onward and upward, soon enough
I move, moved by heavenly puffs . . .

PEISETAIROS

If you don't give over, you'll be permanently out of puff.   1040
*(Peisetairos takes a wing from a basket and beats Kinesias about the
head.)*

KINESIAS

. Now to the south, now to the north I hurry
plowing the ether's furrowless furrow . . .
(puts his hands over his head)

I've had enough of the sound of one wing flapping.

PEISETAIROS

You have, have you? You don't like "moving in every sense"? You
don't like being *kinetic*?

KINESIAS

I hope you realize that I'm a highly renowned chorus master. The
community choirs in Athens are all mad keen to
hire me.

PEISETAIROS

How would you like to stay here and direct a chorus sponsored
by Leotrophides? It's the Duke of Abercorncrake
chorus.

KINESIAS

> I know you're taking the piss out of me. But I'm not going to be
> thwarted in my ambition, I'll have you know, to
> have a pair of wings and to take off from there.
>
> *(Peisetairos has driven Kinesias off the stage, making way for a*
> *supergrouse, who wears a tattered coat.)*

SUPERGROUSE

> "What bird this is I think I know.
> A swallow of patchwork calico."

PEISETAIROS

> Uh oh. Here comes more trouble.   1050

SUPERGROUSE

> "A long-winged swallow of calico."

PEISETAIROS

> Listen to him. He's singing to his coat. It looks as if he'll be glad
> to see a few more swallows.

SUPERGROUSE

> I'm looking for the wing-outfitter.

PEISETAIROS

> You've come to the right place. What do you have in mind?

SUPERGROUSE

> A wing . . . a wing . . . my kingdom for a wing . . .

PEISETAIROS

> If you need some heat and shelter, why don't you head on over to
> Pellene and buy yourself a cloak?

SUPERGROUSE

> It's wings I need. I need them for my work. I'm a summons-
> server.

PEISETAIROS

You mean a supergrouse? Nice work if you can get it.

SUPERGROUSE

Summons-server, supergrouse, stoolpigeon—whatever you call
it, I need wings to keep moving in the right
circles round the provinces, serving summonses
as I go.

PEISETAIROS

Do you think having a pair of wings will make you a superior
summons-server?   1060

SUPERGROUSE

Not exactly, but I'll have less trouble with pirates and privateers.
I'll be able to come back here with the cranes,
though loaded down with writs rather than grit.

PEISETAIROS

What sort of work is this to be involved in? A young man like
yourself? Running around as a paid informer.

SUPERGROUSE

It was the best I could do. I'm not much inclined to manual
labor.

PEISETAIROS

Heavens above. There're so many decent ways of making a living,
ways that are suitable and just, without your
having to resort to adjusting suits.

SUPERGROUSE

I wish you'd stop trying to tell me how I should live my life when
all I want you to give me is a pair of wings.

PEISETAIROS

That's what I am doing. Giving you the wings of words.

SUPERGROUSE
Wings of words?

PEISETAIROS
Everybody takes wing, in a sense, with words.

SUPERGROUSE
Everybody?   1070

PEISETAIROS
Haven't you heard the men sitting around in the barber-shop?
"Ditrephes has allowed my boy's imagination to
take wing," says one, "by letting him think he's
going to be driving around in a custom-built
chariot." Another says that his son is so fired up
by the idea of the theater that he's "transported,"
as it were, by the latest tragedy.

SUPERGROUSE
So it's words that have inspired them?

PEISETAIROS
Of course. It's words that have taken them out of themselves,
uplifted their spirits. That's how I want to exalt
you, to encourage you to turn to some higher
calling.

SUPERGROUSE
I don't want a higher calling.

PEISETAIROS
You don't?

SUPERGROUSE
I don't want to be an embarrassment to my family. My family
have been in the informing business for

generations and generations. So why don't you
just give me a nice pair of racing wings—a
hawk's or a kestrel's, say—and let me get on with
serving a warrant on some illegal alien, fix the
preliminary hearing in this jurisdiction, then
scoot back to Athens.

PEISETAIROS

I get it . . . This way the foreigner will lose the suit even before he
arrives here.

SUPERGROUSE

You *do* get it, don't you?

PEISETAIROS

Then he sails *here* to answer the summons while you fly *there* and
help yourself to his money, right?

SUPERGROUSE

Exactly. I'll be birling back and forth like a top.

PEISETAIROS

Like a top? You know, I think I've got just the job for you.   1080
*(Peisetairos reaches under a heap of wings and pulls out an ivory-
handled, two-tailed, Corcyraean whip.)*
It's a very special pair of wings, in the best Corcyraean dual-
tradition tradition.

SUPERGROUSE

Hoooooooooooooooooooooly Shiiiiiiiiiiiiiiiiiiit. My number's up . . .
It's a split-haired fucking whip.

PEISETAIROS

Whip, nothing . . . It's a pair of wings . . . And I'm going to make
you birl back and forth like a top, all right.
(Peisetairos lashes the Supergrouse with the whip.)

SUPERGROUSE

>Hooooooooooooooooooooly Shiiiiiiiiiiiiiiiiiiiiit.
>It's over. I'm done for.

PEISETAIROS

>Why don't you just birl on out of here? Why don't you just keep
>>on keeping on, you shithead? Otherwise you'll
>>>see some real turning and twisting of the law.
>*(The supergrouse exits hurriedly. Peisetairos turns his attention to*
>>*Xanthias and Manes.)*
>Come on. Let's pack up these wings and go.

CHORUS

>Many weird and wonderful things we see
>as we fly over the fields.
>There is, for instance, an unusual tree   1090
>by the name
>of Cleonymus, the self-same
>who, in spring, issues buds and lawsuits
>and, in winter, throws down his shield
>and quakes in his boots.
>There is, moreover, a land where no lamp shines,
>where gods and mortals together dine,
>but only during daylight hours. For if a mortal should meet
>with the likes of Orestes, Orestes will tan his hide.
>The mortal will be stripped   1100
>of everything from tip
>to toe and left for dead in the street.
>He'll have no sensation in his right side.
>*(Prometheus enters, wrapped in a cloak and carrying a rude umbrella.)*

PROMETHEUS

>Oh dear, dear, dear me. Oh dearie, dearie, dearie me. I hope
>>Zeus doesn't catch sight of me. Where is that
>>>Peisetairos?

PEISETAIROS
 What's up? Who's this doing the muffle-shuffle?

PROMETHEUS
 Do you see a god following me?

PEISETAIROS
 I don't. Who would you be yourself?

PROMETHEUS
 What time of day is it?

PEISETAIROS
 Time? Shortly after noon. Who are you?

PROMETHEUS
 Time to let the oxen out? Or later?   1110

PEISETAIROS
 You know, a body could get sick, sore, and tired of you.

PROMETHEUS
 I wonder what Zeus is doing. Is he clearing the skies or piling
   them up with clouds?

PEISETAIROS
 Are you looking for a good kicking?

PROMETHEUS
 Hold on . . . I'll unwrap my muffler.
 (Prometheus shows his face.)

PEISETAIROS
 Prometheus! My dear friend!

PROMETHEUS

    Wheesht, man . . . Don't talk so loud . . .

PEISETAIROS

    What's the problem, Prometheus?

PROMETHEUS

    Wheesht, I say . . . Don't mention my name. If Zeus finds me
        here, it'll be the end for me. I tell you what. Why
        don't you hold this parasol over my head so the
        gods won't see me from above.

PEISETAIROS

    By heavens . . . You've really thought this through. This is what I
        call forward planning.
    (takes the umbrella and holds it over Prometheus)
    Duck down under here and tell me all.   1120

PROMETHEUS

    Listen to me.

PEISETAIROS

    I am listening. Go on.

PROMETHEUS

    Zeus is done for. It's all over for him.

PEISETAIROS

    Done for? How come?

PROMETHEUS

    Since you established Nebulbulfast, there have been no sacrifices
        to the gods. The smoke of burnt offerings has
        not risen since then. Instead, it's as if we're
        fasting for the festival of Demeter. We've got
        nothing to eat.

Then there are the barbarian gods, the gods of the outlands,
who're starving as well. They're screaming and
shouting like Illyrians and threatening to march
against Zeus unless he agrees to lift our embargo
on exporting roasted guts.

PEISETAIROS
You mean there are *other* gods, barbarians living beyond you?

PROMETHEUS
Of course. If there weren't barbarian gods, to whom would
Exekestides make *his* burnt offerings?

PEISETAIROS
And these barbarian gods, what are they called?

PROMETHEUS
I believe they're known as the Triballi.   1130

PEISETAIROS
Triballi? You mean they're from Triballyslapguttery?

PROMETHEUS
Could be. One thing I know for sure is that you can shortly
expect to see representatives from both Zeus and
the Triballians. Here's my advice. You shouldn't
accept terms and make a peace treaty with
anybody unless Zeus agrees to share power with
the birds and offers you Queen Maybe's hand in
marriage.

PEISETAIROS
Who's Queen Maybe?

PROMETHEUS
She's a lovely, lovely bride-to-be who looks after not only Zeus'
lightning bolt but a number of other things—

> Good Counsel, Good Law, Prudent Behavior, the
> Ship Building Industry, Slagging Matches, the
> National Debt, and the Jurymen's Per Diem
> Authority.

PEISETAIROS
So she's in charge of virtually everything?

PROMETHEUS
> That's what I'm saying. If you can only get her, you've got
> everything. That's why I came here. To let
> you know how things stand, out of my much-
> vaunted generosity of spirit.

PEISETAIROS
> You're the very embodiment of generosity. It's thanks to you,
> after all, that we can fire up our barbecues.

PROMETHEUS
The other thing is, I just *hate* the gods. I just can't abide them.

PEISETAIROS
I know it . . . You're a born god-hater.

PROMETHEUS
> A superlative god-hater . . . A god-hater *par excellence* . . . Now,
> hand me back my parasol, so even if Zeus does
> spot me, he'll take me for an attendant to some
> sacred basket bearer at one of the festivals.   1140
(Peisetairos hands Prometheus a three-legged stool.)

PEISETAIROS
> Why don't you take this loose stool and be a stool bearer as well?
> *(Prometheus slips away under his parasol while Peisetairos prepares to do*
> *some grilling over an open fire.)*

CHORUS

    In the far-flung beat
    of the so-called "Shadowfeet,"
    where a man uses his own hoof
    to put a roof
    over his head, where that most
    foul Socrates summons up ghosts
    by the side of a lake,
    fainthearted, fat Peisander came, hoping to make
    contact with the very soul   1150
    that had fled him, eager to be untrammeled,
    while he was still alive. He had to offer up a whole
    young camel, a whole young camel
    from whose throat, as he cut it, there made
    its way a bat-faced
    Chairephon, instead of his own shade,
    from which he would have shrunk and shied away, in any case.
(Poseidon, Heracles, and the god of the Triballians make a grand
                    entrance. Heracles carries a club. While Poseidon
                    speaks, he tries to rearrange the uncouth god's
                    cloak.)

POSEIDON

    Now we have arrived in Nebulbulfast, the object of our
              mission . . . Hey, God of the Triballians, what's
              your problem? Can't you see you're wearing your
              cloak to the left? Could you change that to the
              right, if you don't mind?
    What's your problem now, you string of misery? Is it that your
              legs are as twisted as Laispodias'? I don't believe
              it . . . This is the inevitable outcome of the
              process of democratization . . . The gods have
              voted the likes of *this* into public office . . .
    Will you stay still for one minute? I have to say that I've come
              across a few culchie gods in my time but nothing
              like this for good old-fashioned culchiness . . .

Anyhow . . . Heracles, what are we going to do
here?   1160

HERACLES

I told you what I want to do. The guy who built the wall and shut
out the gods, I'd like to string him up.

POSEIDON

But we've been sent here to reach a settlement.

HERACLES

That's why stringing him up is the perfect solution.
(Peisetairos wheels out his grill. He's cooking, of all things, birds, assisted
by Xanthias and a wing-wielding Manes.)

PEISETAIROS

Would somebody give me the cheese-grater. And a touch of
silphium. Bring me the cheese, too. Here . . .
fan that flame, would you?

HERACLES

We have the honor, the three of us, gods all, of paying our
respects to the honorable gentleman . . .

PEISETAIROS *(absorbed)*

Can't you see I'm busy grating a little silphium?

HERACLES

What are you cooking there?

PEISETAIROS

Birds, actually. A few that were tried and sentenced to death for
treason. Rebels. They were rebelling against the
Avian League.

HERACLES

So that's why you torture them first. Adding silphium to injury.

PEISETAIROS *(looking up from his work)*
    Oh, Heracles. Hail. What can I do for you? 1170

HERACLES
    We're here as ambassadors from the gods concerning a cease-fire.

PEISETAIROS *(to Xanthias)*
    There's no olive oil in the bottle.

HERACLES *(hungrily rubbing his hands)*
    Bird meat can certainly use plenty of olive oil.

POSEIDON
    We gods have no interest in continuing with the armed struggle.
        As for you, if you were nice to us, we could
        promise you . . . fresh rainwater in your drinking
        puddles and . . . halcyon days in perpetuity. We
        are authorized to negotiate with you in all such
        matters.

PEISETAIROS
    We didn't start this war. We want peace, though peace with
        justice. Zeus must give back his scepter to the
        birds. If you accept these terms, we can all sit
        down immediately and have a spot of lunch.

HERACLES
    That works for me. I'm all in favor of that.

POSEIDON
    Are you crazy? You're being led by your stomach. Are you going
        to allow your father to lose his special position?

PEISETAIROS
    Not at all. Isn't it the case that the gods will be even *more*
        powerful if the birds look after things down
        below? As it is, since they're hidden under the

clouds, eyes to the ground, the humans often
swear false oaths in your names.
If you make a pact with the birds so that a human has to swear
not only "by Zeus" but "by Zeus and a Raven"
and the human breaks his oath, then the raven
can at least swoop down and put out his eye.

POSEIDON
By Poseidon, if I may say, I couldn't have put that better myself. 1180

HERACLES
Sounds good to me.
(*to the god of the Triballians*)
                    What do *you* say?

TRIBALLIAN
Nicey big nicey.

HERACLES
You see? He's for it too.

PEISETAIROS
Let me give you an example of another benefit you can enjoy.
Suppose someone vows to make an offering to a
god, then reneges on it by saying "the gods are
infinitely patient," then we'll collect.

POSEIDON
How so?

PEISETAIROS
Well, when he's counting his money, or lying in his bath, exposed
to the world, a kite will roar down and pick up
the price of a couple of sheep and return it to the
god in question.

HERACLES
Once again, I vote to return the scepter to the birds.

POSEIDON
Let's ask the Triballian what he thinks.

HERACLES *(raising his club threateningly)*
Mister Triballian . . . are you ready for a little assault and battery?

TRIBALLIAN
Nicey, nicey her under. Chickie your lay.   1190

HERACLES
See? He's completely in favor.

POSEIDON
Well, if you're both for it, then it's fine with me.

HERACLES *(to Peisetairos)*
It's a deal. The business of the scepter has been agreed upon.

PEISETAIROS
One other little matter which almost slipped my mind . . . Hera,
              of course, stays with Zeus, but Queen Maybe—
              she must become my wife.

POSEIDON *(taken aback)*
It's quite clear that you have no genuine interest in a settlement.
(to his companions)
Come on. Let's go home.

PEISETAIROS
See if I care.
(to Xanthias)
              Just make sure that sauce is really sweet.

HERACLES

Poseidon, what's got into you? Where do you think you're going? Surely we're not going to fight a war over a single woman?

POSEIDON

What do you suggest?

HERACLES

I suggest we sign a treaty.   1200

POSEIDON

Are you crazy? Can't you see we're being sold short? You're certainly not acting in your own best interest. If Zeus dies after handing back his skepter, *you're* the one who'll have nothing to show for it. Whatever Zeus leaves behind is meant to go to you.

PEISETAIROS *(putting his arm around Heracles)*

He's messing you about. Come over here and let me explain something to you. Your uncle's pulling a fast one on you. You're not legally entitled to any of your father's estate. You're not legitimate. You're, you know . . . a byblow.

HERACLES

Me? A byblow? How do you mean?

PEISETAIROS

I mean that you're the son of a foreign woman, a human. Do you seriously think that Athena would be called the "Heiress of Zeus" if there were legitimate brothers around?

HERACLES

Suppose my father gives me a limited bequest when he dies?

PEISETAIROS

The law won't let him. And Poseidon, here, the one who's egging
you on, would be the very first to contest the will
on the grounds that *he's* a legitimate brother.
Let me quote you Solon's law: "In the case of
there being surviving legitimate children, an
illegitimate child has no right of inheritance; in
the case of there being no legitimate children, the
inheritance shall be shared by the nearest
relatives."

HERACLES

Does that mean I get nothing at all?

PEISETAIROS

Nothing. Has your father ever registered you as a member of
his clan?

HERACLES

Registered me? He hasn't, actually . . .
(A stunned look comes over him, a look of recognition and anger.)
You know, I've been wondering about that . . .   1210

PEISETAIROS

There's no need for you to stare up at the sky with that big, long,
murderous face. I tell you what . . . if you join
forces with us, I'll give you complete control over
the birds . . . the Birds'-milk Marketing Board.

HERACLES

You know what? This thing about Queen Maybe . . . I do believe
I'm in favor of handing her over to you.

PEISETAIROS *(to Poseidon)*

What do *you* say?

POSEIDON
I say no.

PEISETAIROS
It all hangs on the Triballian.
(addressing him)

What do you say?

TRIBALLIAN
Nicey girlum gone big swallies.

HERACLES
He says give her.

POSEIDON
No, he doesn't. He says *don't* give her unless she goes "with the
swallows."

HERACLES
That's right. That's exactly right. She should go "with the
swallows."
(The god of the Triballians nods earnestly.)

POSEIDON
Well, since you two seem to have outvoted me, you should
draw up the terms of the treaty, and I'll just
stay out of it.   1220

HERACLES *(to Peisetairos)*
We've decided to accept your terms. Now you must accompany
us up above so that we can hand over Queen
Maybe and everything else that comes with her.

PEISETAIROS
It's a good thing these birds are already on the grill. They'll be
just perfect for a marriage feast.

HERACLES
   Do you want me to stay behind and oversee the cooking while
            you all go on ahead?

PEISETAIROS
   Leave you in charge? Too risky. You'd better come along with us.

HERACLES
   But I was so well placed to look after all that.

PEISETAIROS *(calling up to the Hoopoe's nest)*
   Could you give me the loan of a wedding outfit, by any chance?
(Peisetairos exits after the trio of gods.)

CHORUS
   On a promontory of Chios,
   by a speech-timer water-clock,
   there's a race of Bellytongues
   who live on talk, talk, talk.   1230
   It's with their tongues
   they sow and reap.
   It's with their tongues
   they harvest figs and grapes.
   But they should think twice,
   Gorgias and Phillipus and all
   those others given to a burst
   of eloquence; in Athens, they might recall,
   when we sacrifice
   an animal, we cut the tongue out first.   1240
(A heavenly runner enters.)

HEAVENLY RUNNER
   O you who prosper more than words can tell, you who are
            blessed in so many ways, ways too numerous to
            recount, prepare to receive your most illustrious
            leader. For he draws near, shining with an

intensity unimaginable even in a star, in a
sunbeam even. He holds a thunderbolt in
his hand.
Beside him is a woman of such radiant beauty it, too, beggars
description. An ineffable fragrance rises
magnificently, incense-smoke wafting
magnificently away on the gentle breeze.
But lo, here comes the man himself. Now let the mouth of the
Muse open and our voices be raised.
*(Peisetairos enters, transformed by his glittering robe, with an equally
glittering Queen Maybe on his arm. The chorus
of birds flutter about the wedding procession,
seemingly untroubled by the fact that Peisetairos
rather than themselves is in charge of Nebulbulfast.
There's more than a faint air of tackiness.)*

CHORUS

Up, up and away, come fly with me around
this happy man who joined with us to found
the beautiful city of Nebulbulfast.
Here's a union that was meant to last.

CHORUS LEADER

What great, good luck
has come to us ducks
through this Peisetairos baby.   1250
And let us limn
a bridal hymn
to his lovely Queen Maybe.

CHORUS

Once the Fates brought Hera and Zeus together,
they sang along like birds of a feather:
Hymen, O, Hymenaeus O
Hymen, O, Hymenaeus O.
And the best man, Eros, checking the reins

of the chariot, continued in that vein: 1260
Hymen, O, Hymenaeus O
Hymen, O, Hymenaeus O.

PEISETAIROS
    I love this hymn. I'm over the moon
    with both the words and the tune.

CHORUS LEADER
    Come celebrate now, too, the jolt
    of Zeus' lightning-flash and thunderbolt.
(The tintinnabulation of an off-stage thunder machine.)

CHORUS
    Behold the lightning flash and thunderbolt of Zeus,
    who once had exclusive use
    of the flash of lightning, the bolt of thunder.
    Not only do they now come under
    the jurisdiction of Peisetairos, but Zeus' late   1270
    ward, Queen Maybe, is now Peisetairos' mate.
    O Hymen. O Hymenaeus O.

PEISETAIROS
    Follow the wedding party, then,
    to the world above.
(reaches out to Queen Maybe)
    Come, my love,
    my little hen,
    let me take you on my pinions
    and bear you away
    to our new dominion
    on this day of days.   1280
*(Peisetairos and Queen Maybe are hoisted heavenward. The chorus
            crowd in, their faces upturned, some cooing, some
            crowing, some clucking in dismay.)*

CHORUS

    Alalalai. Alalalai. Thrum, thrum, thrum.
    Seeseesee the conquering hero come.
    Alalalai. Alalalai.
    Heheheheavens above . . . O heavens above.

About the Translators

GREG DELANTY'S latest poetry collection is *The Hellbox*; his earlier volumes are *American Wake*, *Southward*, and *Cast in the Fire*. His poems have appeared in the United States, Ireland, England, and Australia in anthologies such as the *Field Day Anthology of Irish Writing* and the *Norton Introduction to Poetry* as well as magazines and journals such as the *Atlantic Monthly*, *New Statesman*, *Irish Times*, and *Times Literary Supplement*. He edited, with Nuala Ní Dhomhnaill, *Jumping Off Shadows: Selected Contemporary Irish Poets* and, with Robert Welch, *New and Selected Poems of Patrick Galvin*. His numerous honors include the Patrick Kavanagh Award, the Allen Dowling Poetry Fellowship, the Wolfers-O'Neill Award, the Austin Clark Award, and an Arts Council of Ireland Bursary. He was born in Cork, Ireland and lives in Burlington, Vermont, where he teaches at St. Michael's College.

RICHARD MARTIN, a specialist in Greek literature, mythology, and religion, received his A.B. and Ph.D. degrees from Harvard University. Since 1981 he has taught in the Classics Department at Princeton University, since 1994 as Professor of Classics. His books include an edition of *Bulfinch's Mythology* and *The Language of Heroes: Speech and Performance in the Iliad*.

PAUL MULDOON is the author of 19 volumes of original poetry, most recently *Kerry Slides*, *New Selected Poems, 1968–1994*, *The Annals of Chile*, *The Prince of the Quotidian*, and *Incantata*. He has translated from the Irish *The Astrakhan Cloak*, by Nuala Ní Dhomhnaill. He has written two operas (*Vera of Las Vegas*, *Shining Brow*), two plays (*Six Honest Serving Men*, *Monkeys*, which was broadcast by the BBC in 1989), and three books for children. His work is represented in such major anthologies of Irish and British poetry as *The Penguin Book of Contemporary British Poetry*, *The Penguin Book of Contemporary Irish Poetry*, and *The Norton Anthology of Mod-*

ern Poetry (second edition). His work has earned him the T. S. Eliot Prize, the Sir Geoffrey Faber Memorial Award (twice), a John Simon Guggenheim Memorial Fellowship, and the Eric Gregory Award. He is a member of Aosdana and a fellow of the Royal Society of Literature. He has taught at the University of Massachusetts, Amherst College, University of California at Berkeley, Columbia University, University of East Anglia, and Cambridge University. He is currently Howard G. B. Clark Professor in the Humanities and Director of the Creative Writing Program at Princeton University.

CAROL POSTER is the author of three volumes of poetry— *Blackbird, Deceiving the Worms,* and *Surrounded by Dangerous Things*—and two books of humorous commercial nonfiction. Her translations include Plautus' *Stichus* (in the Complete Roman Drama in Translation series) and *Selected Poems of Jacques Prévert.* Her poetry also appears frequently in literary periodicals such as *Literacy Review, Riverrun, Wisconsin Review, Kansas Quarterly, Bitterroot,* and *The Formalist.* Her scholarly articles on rhetoric, philosophy, and literature have appeared in *Philosophy and Rhetoric, Rhetoric Society Quarterly, College English, Pre/text, Mystics Quarterly,* and other journals. She won the 1997 Gildersleeve Prize for best article in *American Journal of Philology.* She has taught at the University of Northern Iowa and is currently Associate Professor of English at Montana State University.

9 780812 216981